EDITORIAL

This volume begins with two papers on the theme of holding. Jessica James, in her paper "The Application of Group Analysis in the Childbearing Year: the function of holding", uses her experience as a group conductor of parents with new-born infants, and as a birth attendant, to show that in order for the mother to be able to hold her infant she herself needs to feel held by a parental figure. Professor Renata Gaddini's paper on "Lullabies and Rhymes in the Emotional Life of Children" looks at an aspect of holding through the mother's singing of lullabies and other songs to her infant. Her paper draws on and follows on from an earlier paper, "The Precursors of Transitional Objects and Phenomena", published in *Winnicott Studies*, volume 1, 1985.

The two following papers attempt to throw more light on Winnicott's thinking on the use of an object and on the transference. Laurel Samuels, in her paper "A Historical Analysis of Winnicott's 'The Use of an Object'", investigates the circumstances, and the effect on Winnicott himself, of his first public account of his concept of the use of an object, at a lecture given to the New York Psychoanalytic Society in 1968. My own paper, "Winnicott and Transference: the knife-edge of belief", takes an historical and critical look at the concept of transference, and attempts to flesh out what is distinctive in Winnicott's understanding of transference.

The two final contributions are intended to mark the fact that *Winnicott Studies* is changing from a journal to a series of books (described below), which means that this is the last volume of *Winnicott Studies* in its present form. In her paper "A First Approach to clinical work . . . taken by the hand of Winnicott", Carolina Castro attempts to tell two stories: of her clinical work with a young boy, and of her own work in turning Winnicott into a form of mentor and inspiration for her, rather as she became for her client. *Winnicott Studies* was always intended as a spur for readers to use their own imagination and critical sensibility in order to allow themselves to be "taken by the hand of Winnicott", wherever that might take them.

This volume ends with an anthology of poems, collected for us by Anthony Rudolf. Winnicott was, I think, distrustful of technical and abstract language for the description and understanding of human life, although he was obliged to use it himself. He held creative artists in high esteem, believing they could often express much of what he wanted to say about human development better than he could himself, and several of his papers detail how he came upon some of his ideas out of a prolonged dialogue with, say, a series of paintings or a particular poem. It thus seems fitting to end with a contribution which is not in the usual academic style of the journal, but which hopefully complements it in its direct appeal to the imagination of the reader.

As I have said, this is the last volume of *Winnicott Studies* in its present format, and also the last with myself as editor. The journal is in the process of being transformed into book form, with individual volumes being published with papers on specific themes bearing directly or indirectly on Winnicott's work. The new editor is Val Richards, with Gillian Wilce as assistant editor. It only remains for me to wish them well, and to thank the editorial committee and editorial consultants to the journal, and all those in the Squiggle Foundation, as well as all those who have contributed to the journal, for their hard work and dedication which have made *Winnicott Studies* possible.

THE APPLICATION OF GROUP ANALYSIS IN THE CHILD-BEARING YEAR: THE FUNCTION OF HOLDING

Jessica James

INTRODUCTION

Child-Birth as Linked to All Phases of Child-Bearing

In this paper I am looking at how women and their partners may be helped to use the transformations of pregnancy and childbirth to prepare for looking after a small baby and being a parent. Significantly there is no word to describe the totality of this phase and in our culture they tend to be regarded separately. Breen (1985) shares this view. I see them as inextricably linked and as a powerful period with enormous potential for growth and change. I shall call this phase the child-bearing year, to cover the woman's responses to pregnancy, to childbirth, to the early months of motherhood. In pregnancy there tends to be a focus on the birth as an isolated event with little relation to any of the other experiences and of enormous dread, foreboding and fear "to be survived". I want to discuss the possibility that the labour is, in fact, not isolated but the most intense, regressive metaphor for the holding needed by the labouring woman, akin to that which the new baby also requires.

Birth Attending and Analytic Practice

I have developed my ideas through experience and practice as a birth attendant. A birth attendant, as I see it, is distinct from other persons caring for a labouring woman in that she has some professional detachment and expertise, is there solely to support the woman through the intense experience of labour and has no medical responsibility. I intend to draw on my experiences in this field in the first section. I will be suggesting that the importance of child-bearing stands at the centre of all analytic practice. At the heart of the analytic experience lies a recreation

3

of our most regressive infantile needs for attention to the non-verbal, metaphorical experiences of "being with" and "being held". The analytic clients' own history will be lived through and regarded retrospectively and suppositiously. I am seeking to develop a practice and a range of ideas to help practically with the primary and fundamental experience of birth. In this way, I am applying and interchanging the concepts of analytic practice with child-bearing, so as to formulate an approach which recognises the emotional significance of the phases and their potential for prevention and well-being.

Groups in a Life Transition

The second section will describe how groups offered during the child-bearing year can provide the opportunity to recognize and mark this life change, so that both men and women can live it, not just survive it and become able to tolerate and allow the rollercoaster of emotions that pregnancy, child-birth and a new baby bring.

Women, sometimes men, come to child-birth preparation groups having never been to groups before. Overtly these groups have a potential for intimacy which is, perhaps, the benign mother group perceived in positive non-conflictual terms that Sheidlinger (1974) suggests. Covertly they may also have a more therapeutic potential that involves acknowledging the painful, conflictual elements of change, adaptation and threats of engulfment. In joining these groups there isn't the stigma of having failed that psychotherapy suggests to so many people; in fact there are overtones of success. in our society becoming a parent represents the joyous and romanticised notions of the "family" and "motherhood". Yet whilst having a baby can mean fulfilment and normality, just below the surface also lie more ambivalent feelings and doubts. For women, in particular, there lies the fear of never being herself again, of losing the self she knows, being a mother rather than a woman and a major change to her body, self image and life-style. For men there are also changes, especially if he wants to become an involved rather than a distant father. In our society most women and men have little or no experience of babies before they get pregnant and tend to be separate from their families of origin and extended family support. There is an acknowledged need for support through this life crisis and such groups replace the rituals and structure of women's shared lives together which are a part of some societies that we regard as primitive. They provide an opportunity for mourning the loss of the past life and preparing for the new life. They have enormous therapeutic potential at a time when people feel churned up, open and available to their inner worlds. As such they are an opportunity to find the baby inside each other and, by bringing it into the open, going some way to having it attended to and understood. As Skynner (1983) writes:

> there is nearly always care and affection available if people ask for it . . . it's their attitude that stops them receiving affection . . . as their baby is shut away behind that tightly held-down screen.

Being a parent and joining a group to prepare for birth is a socially acceptable way for people going through a life crisis to develop alongside their babies.

THE BIRTH EXPERIENCE

I am going to start by describing the experience of women in labour because it is in this context that one can see most accurately how her regression and need for holding enables, at a later stage, her ability to empathise with her baby. They highlight the mechanisms that operate throughout the child-bearing year. In this section I want to examine how the labour itself provides an intensive, regressive experience comparable to the new baby's. I have developed in my role as a birth attendant, in hearing stories of labours and in my work preparing for child-birth, an increasing awareness of the link between the labouring woman's needs with the baby's. In my reading of psychoanalytic literature this has been borne out, in descriptions of mother-baby interactions, as well as the analogies of the importance of the environment and non-verbal cues provided by the analytic situation. I want to suggest that child-birth may be an opportunity for women to identify with a re-experience being a baby as a preparation for motherhood. Winnicott (Davis and Wallbridge, 1981, p, 94) writes of this:

> In the weeks before and after the birth of the baby, the mother and baby share certain experiences. These strengthen the mother's identification with the baby and result in the "experience of mutuality"—the birth itself . . . is the feeling of being in the grip of something external, so that one is helpless .. there is a very clear relation here between what the baby experiences in being confined, as it is called. There comes a state in the labour in which, in health, a mother has to resign herself to a process almost exactly comparable to the infant's experience at the same time.

The Body in Labour
Somatic Regression

During the child-bearing year a woman's body will undergo enormous changes which will attract her own and others attention. Different women will cope with this according to their attitude to their bodies and their own previous history. Somatic expressions of emotional pain are common and compounded by the medical care she receives which tends to emphasise the nuances of her physicality. Since our very first self-awareness in infancy is somatic and our first ego is a body ego, a woman's intense awareness of her body at this time will generate regressive and infantile feelings (Raphael-Leff 1991).

Attending to a woman in labour involves constant contact with her body on the most basic level. Her excremental functions, body temperature, emission of fluids, needs for nourishment, energy levels are to the fore along with her contracting uterus. Responding on a physical level involves mopping up, soothing, providing containers, changing clothes, feeding and giving drinks, rocking and breathing together.

One woman, in the late stages of labour, felt the need to sit on the loo. We walked slowly towards it with my arms around her shoulders. We stopped for contractions and stood with her leaning against the wall, with me holding her hips, swaying and breathing deeply together, then we proceeded to the toilet. Before we got there, she felt sick and I found a bowl in which she vomited. At the toilet she sat on it but lost the need to go. She became very cold and we walked back to the labour room, dealing with the contractions in the same way against the wall. In between contractions I found a blanket to put round and woolly socks to put on. Amniotic fluid was dripping from her vagina, which seemed distressing to her and I helped to mop it up; the midwife found a clean towel and pants. She started to feel like pushing, the midwife cleaned away faeces. The labouring woman leant over my shoulders and bore down. She felt hot, I helped to take off everything she wore. In between contractions I sponged down her face with a cold sponge. One time I didn't cool the sponge and she directed me to do so . . .

Doing the Thinking for Her

These minute by minute, moment by moment, details of attention to her physical needs, in this instance, are like those required by a small baby. Although a woman obviously has the potential to give verbal explanations of what she wants, in fact it is a hindrance and effort to have to find the words. To articulate with words involves denying her regressive experience and above all what she wants is to have someone linked into her non-verbal cues and to do the thinking for her. With attention paid to her bodily requirements in this way, she gets confirmation that her body is healthy, doing the right things, is not shocking nor repugnant to others.

Many women feel contempt for their body, estranged from its functions and processes, often generated by the way their body was regarded and treated when they were young. The experience of birth (along with the whole child-bearing period although birth as the most intense manifestation) may be an opportunity to re-introject positive feelings about her body, which she may or may not have received from her early experiences.

Skin Communication

The childbirth provides a normal, developmental phase for women to re-experience bodily, soothing contact. Pines D. (1980) describes patients who have found psychosomatic solutions to psychic pain with skin disorders requiring physical contact through touching and soothing where verbal communication is blocked. She calls this "skin communication". She suggests that the skin as a medium for physical contact represents a boundary of self and non-self. In cases where the mother has handled the baby through its skin in a non-containing, negative and anxious way, this results in the baby's affects finding expression through disorders of the skin. The stroking massaging skin to skin contact of childbirth given by a containing, confident attendant can be seen as analogous to that which may be transmitted as a source of pleasure and intimacy between mother and baby. The labouring woman can internalise this experience and not have to re-seek it through psychosomatic expressions later.

Breathing in Labour

Breathing, also a bodily experience, is a powerful part of the labour and a direct link with the baby as well. We could say that breathing together in labour is a dyadic song without words. The contact made is through taking the sound and feel of the breath, playing with it by finding a rhythm together, sometimes making slight alterations to pitch, tune or level of sound, but always as a response to the labouring woman's own creation. So I have found myself in labours getting into all sorts of rhythms and sounds of breathing, sometimes with a sense of desperation, at other times quite tuneful. The kind of breathing that I encourage women to use is deep belly breathing, that babies do naturally when they are born. The stomach of a baby expands and contracts with their breath as the oxygen flows in and the lungs fill completely and deeply. This is lost as we grow up and become hurried, tense and shallow with our breath.

Images of Labour

A stereotypical portrayal of labour is of a shrill screaming woman fighting and flailing with the contractions. It is an image of fear and flight (and unfortunately the reality for many women). Deep belly breathing is about accepting and going with the contractions, using the out-breath to breath into them, to soften, relax, open and maximise the oxygen taken in by completely emptying the lungs with each breath. Women are encouraged to make noises with the out-breath, humming, moaning, groaning noises to extend it and to express the feelings. The breathing is also a means of cutting out her thoughts. Her adult capacity to plan can make the experience of labour difficult because there are no rules or clear indications to go by and no-one knows how long it will last. Babies naturally live in the present and have no inhibitions about making noises if they feel like it. At labours, partners are encouraged to keep contact with the labouring women through breathing together. There are other ways, of course, of keeping contact, but this is consistently one of the most helpful. Winnicott (1987) describes the very subtle kinds of needs that babies have and which can only be met by human contact. He includes the involvement in the mother's breathing rhythm as one of them.

> Many times at labours I have been breathing with a woman, so she can hear and feel my breath, only to realise how important this has been if I have momentarily stopped, to be pulled back; "breathe" one woman shouted. Afterwards she said how important it was to have the feel of my breath on her chest and to have me linked into her rhythm of breathing at the same time and pace.

Inevitable Failures

Babies cannot put words to that experience of being let down, but someone in touch with them will realise they have got it wrong and will attempt to mend their failure. Winnicott (Davis and Wallbridge, 1981) talks of failures being necessary for the mother's reliability to be communicated to her infant and in the course of ordinary care a mother is all the time mending her failures. In the same way birth partners will fail occasionally but there is always the possibility of remedy and with adaptation a sense of security and trust in their care.

MIRRORING AND AFFIRMATION

To return to breathing, I want to describe the use of mirroring and affirmation which breathing provides and which is also so important for the confirmation of self for a baby. There are various means of mirroring during labour, such as visually through facial gestures or through moving together. Breathing is one example whereby breathing and making sounds with someone else can provide a profound kind of connectedness crucial to feeling a sense of self during labour. Wright (1991) describes the early dialogue between mother and baby which is through conversations of smiles and gestures. He tells of the significance for the baby of looking and he distinguishes between "interrelated looking" and "looking at". In the same way we could talk of "interrelated breathing" and "breathing at". Interrelated looking involves the mother responding with life-enhancing variations towards the baby's original actions. As such, the response is to take what the baby offers and translate it with a different mode. On the other hand, "looking at" reflects more what the mother is feeling, it is an imposition for the baby who becomes an object and who is left with an atrophied relationship. There is no confirmation of self and the baby will be liable to develop a false self in order to try to please the mother. Wright talks of the rediscovery of the dyadic dance and interactions involved with the rhythmic interchange which say "I like what you've just done and this is what it has done to me".

"Breathing at" would be to do with a failure to respond to the labouring woman's own breath.

One example is when I attempted to make a connection with a woman in labour that I hadn't met before. She was in strong labour, I tried breathing with her as I usually do, she said "don't breath all over my face". It took some time for me to gain her trust, through holding, rocking and mopping down with sponges, before we could connect through the breath which ultimately we did, making low, deep noises together.

Clearly my original attempt had been premature and experienced as an imposition, although in this case, luckily, she had not felt the need to please me and use a false self. The link between Wright's mother and baby dyadic dance and the use of mirroring in labour could be developed in other areas, perhaps mostly in moving together or literally dancing together. Sometimes we rock with a baby in distress and we rock ourselves when in pain. Women in labour find their own movements and by having them responded to and confirmed, perhaps with a variation, again experience a communication where words are not possible.

HOLDING IN LABOUR

Human Context

Winnicott (in Phillips 1988, p. 5) said there is no such thing as a baby:

> if you show me a baby you certainly show me also someone caring for a baby, or at least a pram with someone's eyes and ears glued to it. One sees a nursing couple.

The same applies to a woman in labour. She needs someone to be in tune with her and constantly there for her. Left alone, the experience becomes one of deprivation or even abuse (as it would be for a baby). Individual women's past histories and psychological make-ups will determine the use they are able to make of those trying to help them. It is not the purposes of this paper to look at individual psychopathology. However, I also don't want to deny the reality for many women of the institutionalized abusive care that does exist (Menzies 1961). Kitzinger (1992, p. 109) contrasts hospitals in the West with some traditional cultures. In Western hospitals birth is often a lonely experience with contact reduced to obtaining information or the administering of technological devices,

> the touching has no emotional component and no energy has passed from the helper to the woman in labour.

In traditional cultures:

> birth is almost invariably interactive and involves close and sustained contact to give comfort and encouragement to relieve pain ... in some cultures the midwife is known as "the woman who holds".

Kitzinger is probably referring to physical holding but now I want to develop the idea of holding to include the emotional holding which is in my view crucial for the woman's experience of labour.

Gorillas

Before describing the significance of emotional holding in this context and developing my theme of the potential in the birth for strengthening a woman's sense of self and her capacity to empathise with her baby, I want to mention a research finding. The argument for ending isolation in labour has a powerful force if one looks at some findings based in ethology. Verkes (Kitzinger, 1992, p. 165) found in his research centre that one-third of gorillas cared for their young whilst the other two-thirds either ignored or beat their up. At first he thought this was because they had been captured as infants, but it turned out to be because the two-thirds who were rejecting had been socially isolated during their labours. It was the third who had a cage-mate during labour and birth who cared for their young.

Life or Death Experience

On an emotional level, labour is one of the most intensely powerful experiences that women have. The range and breadth of feelings, the breakdown of defences, the fears and passions aroused, are enormous. At times it can literally feel like life or death. The extent to which a woman feels held and tolerated during this time will influence her capacity to feel strengthened in her own acknowledgement of herself as someone who has needs that can be expressed and met.

Empathy and Empowerment

At moments in attending a woman in labour it can be as though nothing you do is right. She screams, shouts and rejects everything you offer. She stomps around the room with you following, you offer a sponge, strokes, some water but she pushes you away. You try to remember how important you are as a container for all those feelings, perhaps like a parent (or therapist) tries to be, without retaliation. You stay there, do your best, tell her that you are there for her and remind her that it is usual to find it hard at times during labour. Sometimes that difficult patch eases and you become able to make contact and to find a way to comfort. Or it may not be until afterwards that you realise in discussion, that your presence was crucial in enabling her to express those feelings, to find ways of stomping and dealing with the pain in her own way. You discover how important it was that you didn't become overtly anxious, you didn't deny her feelings, nor try to offer her solutions such as drugs, even though you wavered in your own mind at the time. All this seems to have been crucial for her sense of feeling safe and able to let go.

At one labour, a woman said a few times that she wanted to die. Her partner felt awful, yet continued to rock and moan with her and to assure her of his presence. Afterwards she said that the worst part of the labour had been early on in the antenatal ward when alone. When he asked about when she had said she wanted to die, she retorted "oh no, you were there then".

Presumably, he had been someone she could trust sufficiently to hold her emotionally, that she felt heard, acknowledged and looked after. When she was alone there had been no-one to give her that sense of security and her internal resources felt depleted, even though the labour pains would have been, physiologically speaking, less strong in the early stages.

Fear of Emotionality

In a recent Guardian article Orbach (1993) discusses how we are so often
frightened by each other's "emotional productions" that we are also unable to take responsibility for our own. She links this to how we may care
for a baby's distress. Frequently, our alarm or anxiety teaches a baby that
its emissions, its self, is somehow not right.

> A care-giver who has the ability to tolerate a baby's stress, to receive it
> without being frightened, to accept it as valid and at the same time render
> it back to the baby as manageable and understandable, makes it possible
> for the baby to settle ... it can have its feelings without overwhelming
> another or being overwhelmed itself.

Being Saved

I have also referred to Pines' (1980) findings about the ways bodily suffering can represent a translation of psychic pain as a result of a lack of
containment. My descriptions of holding in labour compare to the baby's
need for containment of bodily suffering. Winnicott (1987, p. 86) talks of
the anxieties that babies are likely to feel, which are the most severe that
can be imagined. One of Winnicott's abilities is to put himself into a
baby's mind and to give words to what babies feel. He uses expressions
such as "going to pieces", "falling for ever", "dying and dying and dying", "losing all vestiges of hope of the renewal of contacts". I find these
descriptions fascinating because they have all, in one way or another,
been used by women talking of their labours (again also by women referring to being new mothers).

However, it is the experience of contrast; of being saved, of finding
control, of being alive, maybe also, in this instance, of the baby being
born that makes it all possible. As Winnicott (1987, p. 86) says,

> With good care these awful feelings become good experiences adding up
> to a total of confidence in people and in the world also (the object only
> becomes real by being hated; the infant can only find the world around
> him substantial through his ultimately unsuccessful attempts to destroy
> it).

Need to Please

I have noticed that women who have found their labours most traumatic
or difficult are those who have not felt able to trust anyone sufficiently to
lose control or to allow the powerful feelings to take over. Perhaps they

have felt the need to please, to retain a sense of dignity or to accept the process as inevitably agonizing in a masochistic way, all characteristic mechanisms for women. Most significantly, there may not have been any-one available to perform the function of "holding" for whatever reason, her own capacity to "ask" and or the partner's or midwife's sensitivity to recognise and give. In the final section I shall illustrate how groups can facilitate this.

ENVIRONMENTAL INFLUENCES

Sensitivity to Impingement

I am going to conclude this section on the experience of labour, with some discussion of the environment. As I see it, the environment is the wider context in which the necessary physicality, anxiety and churning up, that I have described, takes place. I will continue to refer to labour but again it could be applied to the whole child-bearing year. I want to con-sider the woman's need for reliability, simplicity and minimal interruption during labour. It is to do with providing a context free of complications and impingements because there is so much going on in-side the woman herself and she is so acutely aware. Nitsun (1989) when he writes of the early development in a group, suggests that at this stage the group is comparable to an infant struggling to achieve a sense of being and unity, that issues of survival are crucial, with fragmentation and disintegration experienced as real anxieties and that, indeed, the lev-els of anxiety may be psychotic in nature. These descriptions tie in with mine of those of the woman in labour. Nitsun suggests the importance for the group of the conductor's sensitivity:

> to avoid forcing premature activity or "impingement" similar to a moth-er's intrusion into the quiescent, formless state of the infant, with the same potentially damaging consequences that produce a precocious or "false development".

I am suggesting that a similar sensitivity is crucial for the labouring woman. Frequently, I have known or have heard of women coping (or maybe only just) with their labours, to be interrupted by a newcomer. The new person, however sensitive, cannot have any idea of the nuances of her needs.

Information and Illusion

Or alternatively the woman in labour is examined, in order to get informa-tion about the baby or her progress. This brings her into the external world and she finds herself collapsing, feeling unable to continue and disintegrating.

One example is when a partner left the room to get a cushion and returned within minutes to find her feeling abandoned and pleading for help. Another is of an internal examination to check cervical dilatation, whereby the woman has to be still, get into a suitable position and be given information.

Again, she loses confidence when she is interrupted and furthermore encouraged to apply her mind and knowledge to the information she is given, such as in working out the anticipated length of labour. If this is longer than she hoped, often she loses faith even though beforehand she had it. Perhaps this is because she has mobilised her intellect and stopped trusting her bodily sensations. If the information has been positive it can serve as a boost, but predictions in labour are often wrong.

A final example is where the professionals are concerned about the baby or the labour's progress which makes it difficult for the woman to concentrate on her own needs.

Intrusions are unavoidable but simplification, protection and continued holding is essential. Winnicott (Phillips, 1988, p. 84) talks of "sustaining the infant's capacity for illusion" for as long as possible. I can relate to Winnicott's reported obliviousness to the external world during the blitz whilst he was analysing psychotic patients (Phillips, 1988). Sometimes, during labours (particularly if there are few impingements) I find day moves into night, time becomes meaningless and there can be a sense of being at the centre of the world. Not so easy if it is your daily work but for the labouring woman (and her partner) that feeling can be a significant marker for remembering the event which produces their baby.

THE GROUP EXPERIENCE

Types of Groups

Before describing the group experience, I want to mention the types of groups I've been concerned with, the role of men and the contribution of professionals.

I offer a package of groups, or classes, which can be attended for about a year, continuing longer in self-help form. I don't want to detail their content, nor emphasise their differences, rather I want to suggest and consider their overall themes and ethos. I offer five types of groups:

(1) On going slow-open "roll on roll off" groups of yoga for pregnant women.

(2)   Closed membership eight week course for women with their partners, usually men.

(3)   One evening class for women and partners (who haven't attended the course but the pregnant woman comes to the yoga).

(4)   Closed membership six week postnatal discussion group for women.

(5)   On going slow-open "roll on roll off" groups of yoga for postnatal women.

Women come to all or some of these groups. I recommend all to first-time mothers but realise that for various reasons this won't always be possible. Women having subsequent babies generally come to the yoga only and the one evening partners class. There develops a culture of understanding and learning offered through myself as dynamic administrator but crucially also through the group.

Gender

Most of what I am discussing in this paper refers to the experience of women but I don't want to under-estimate the potential and importance of men as a systemic part of the couple and family. In fact, the enormity of what a prospective father takes on as the source of care and holding for the pregnant, labouring and postnatal woman needs to be acknowledged and supported. Hopefully, if he joins a group this may, in part, fulfil the role of recognition and preparation for the significance and scale of his contribution.

In the early days of feminism men were encouraged to take on previously ascribed female roles in the home in order to "liberate" women from their drudgery, low status and constraints. Nowadays there is possibly a greater recognition of the value of biological difference, the acceptance of women's natural capacity to child-bear and mother, as a celebration rather than a chattel. Yet men are usually the labouring women's main birth partner and they become involved in child-birth preparation courses. The current climate is shifting regarding men's role in child-birth, with important questions being raised. Whilst, on the one hand, men are increasingly wanting to understand women's and babies' needs, to be involved and to "mother", on the other hand, many men find it hard to empathise, to be truly useful and have a tendency to take over, control and "muscle-in" on what is an essentially womanly experience. It is a complicated issue relating to the whole structure of society, since most babies are born into nuclear families and the majority of women have male partners for their primary support before, during and after the birth. It is, therefore, crucial that the father is involved and has some understanding of their partner's and baby's needs at this time. There is no hope of increased understanding if he doesn't. However, this can only begin with men recognising their own needs, acknowledging their experiences in full and feeling a part of the whole process.

In some cultures there are customs such as "couvade" to encourage men's association with the maternal role, drawing him into identification with the baby, being pampered and sharing in the infant's glory, rather than staring in jealous resentment (Raphael-Leff, 1991, p. 154). In Western cultures some studies (Kitzinger, 1992) have shown men to suffer an increased incidence of psychological disturbance and psychosomatic symptoms, a non-formalised form of couvade which indirectly invites care and attention.

Below, I shall illustrate how the group's year may contribute towards fulfilling this function and acknowledging "couvade" in our culture today.

The Influence of Professionals

The politics of child-birth includes the wider social context in which women have babies including the care offered by professionals. As I have already discussed, child-birth in our society has become medicalised; most women go to hospital for their care which is out of sight, distant and aseptic. Birth is not part of our life and women experiencing it are expected to separate themselves and "suffer" in private. Doctors, who are usually men, dominate with most research funding and interests concentrated upon technological and interventionalist advances. There is some recent recognition of women's choice for increased midwifery involvement, women with women, a "hands-on", non-medical approach. (Winterton, 1992). However, most women are still cared for in a place reserved for illness and death, regarded as in need of specialised, mechanical attention amongst strangers.

Defences against Exposure

In my experience Menzies's (1961) descriptions of defensive techniques in the nursing service apply today almost as much as they did 30 years ago. In many maternity units midwives are encouraged to minimise attachments to people in their care, defer to authority, make few autonomous decisions and remain cut-off from their own feelings. This is in situations of daily contact with the raw emotions for child-birth, repeated exposure to pain, blood, mess and naked emotionality and urgency. Nevertheless, in some situations midwives are working in teams which encourage and support their involvement, personal initiative and recognition of emotional needs. These, in turn, make it possible for individualised and humane care to their clients but benefiting from this kind of care can be an accident of geography, otherwise she will need to be assertive to get what she wants or, alternatively, be able to pay. On the whole the split which exists regarding child-birth, between mystification, scientific understanding and lay women's "ignorance" renders people having babies susceptible to compliance. A woman's submissive obedience, her need to believe in powerful authority figures is convenient in fulfilling the political aim of medicalising child-birth. I have considered here the gap between what tends to be provided by professions in our society for women in the child-bearing year and, as I see it, what their emotional needs demand.

DEVELOPING IN GROUPS

I have given a flavour of the experiences women have in labour. With this as background I now intend to illustrate how belonging to a group can be a helpful preparation. My groups, or classes as they are also known, are an application of group analysis using many of its concepts and ideas. However, they have a more clearly defined education goal; they work with an apparently homogenous group and include physical as well as emotional holding. Such groups have been recognised as a dynamic force in this field of child-birth for some time through National Child-birth Trust and Active Birth. I have my own practice from which I will use examples and which has developed increasingly along group analytic lines.

The Group as the "Ultimate" Mother

Groups are frequently described in terms of their maternal functions, the "Group-as-Mother" (Hearst, 1981). The Matrix is a term initiated by Foulkes and used to describe the web or network of relationships or communications in a group. It derives from Latin for a pregnant or female animal and in later Latin, the womb. Its definitions can be seen to be female, containing and supportive. (Roberts, 1982). Prodgers (1990) suggests the group acts as a representative of the Great Mother containing essential ambivalence. This was clearly the case when I gave a talk to student midwives:

> I mentioned that labouring women could benefit from mothering. They seemed to be appalled at the idea, apparently regarding mothers solely in negative terms and wanting to dissociate themselves from the role. This

reaction brought home to me the strong reactions to mothering that young women and, furthermore, trainee midwives can have.

Groups which are for child-bearing women and men, in particular, suggest a maternal quality. Their very concern is for the quintessentially female experience of having a baby. The teacher is always a woman and mother herself and the group she has created represents a place to find support, understanding and skills to move through this transformation from pregnancy to motherhood. Raphael-Leff (1991, p. 113) writes:

> As in many therapeutic groups, the leader represents a mothering figure and the group itself represents a mother or maternal "breast". In a pregnancy group those metaphors are particularly salient as focal preoccupations revolve around the themes of containing, nurturing and merging.

Group Membership: Diversity

People coming to groups will have their own internal representations and models of "mother". Although the groups may be homogenous in terms of pregnancy, there are variations in terms of age and background. For instance, some members could be in their early twenties, in recently-formed relationships with insecure housing and employment, whilst others may be in their forties in long-term marriages, with successful careers, a mortgage and a history of fertility problems. Most will be from situations somewhere in between. There are unsupported women, younger women, lesbians or women and men from different ethnic groups. However, each will have their own notions of mothering and will bring these with them in their internal worlds. Whilst "mother" can suggest warm, sustaining and nourishing, it can also engender depriving, painful, engulfing images. Some members will bring split metaphors, seeing the group in terms of one or the other: good or bad, idealised or devouring.

Many group members may well be functioning in a paranoid–schizoid way in relation to mothering and, since the very content of the group is to prepare for ourselves as "mother", splitting mechanisms are likely to be especially potent. Someone who has not reached a depressive position will be struggling at the outset with their forthcoming birth. The group is likely to revive difficult feelings and be threatening in its representations. However, most participants will be functioning within the range of "normality", albeit facing a life crisis and an upheaval in their identity, whether or not they are aware of it.

As I see it, it is not the aim of these groups to explore individual's inner worlds, in fact it could be dangerous and exploitative to do so in a situation which does not involve the usual therapeutic boundaries nor have such a stated aim. However, the group does have therapeutic potential in its recognition, acceptance and holding of the range of feelings involved. Schindler (Hearst, 1981) says that in group therapy it is an aim to reduce the fear of the mother, so that the mother group also loses its frightening aspect as does mother society. Prodgers (1990) concurs with this:

> The aim of therapy is to reduce the negative and frightening aspects of mother image.

If this is the aim of heterogenous patient therapy groups, then it must surely be high on the agenda for groups working with people in preparation for child-bearing.

How the Group May Be Used by Different People: Two Examples

Two examples will illustrate the kinds of expectation and aspiration that can be presented by people in groups at their outset. I hope to elucidate the unstated, unconscious emotional expressions towards "mother" and how by belonging to the group these can gradually become acknowledged.

Intellectualising

There is the wish for control by having information and knowledge about the birth (also the pregnancy and baby). This may present itself with detailed questioning over the mechanics of breathing; its physiology, its logic and rationale as well as how to use it in exact terms. I don't encourage this type of discussion as I see it as a flight from facing the preverbal needs of the group which link with its maternal function. At the same time it is important not to alienate group members.

There was a couple, Rose and John, who were both lawyers and on the mental plane as opposed to the emotional or physical. There was a moment when I demonstrated relaxation breathing and was challenged by Rose saying she had read that one could hyperventilate by breathing deeply. Wanting to get away from the "head stuff" I had the problem of getting Rose to trust me and this took several sessions. It finally happened because their awkwardness was accepted and not highlighted in any way. The rest of the group took the breathing and relaxation seriously because of my ease and belief in it. It, therefore, became increasingly difficult for Rose and John to stand around talking about breathing, rather than giving it a try. Through this they were also gently pushed into realms of being with each other that they had never experienced before—they, perhaps, learnt more than any in the group about their own feelings, sensitivities and especially about the individuality of experience. This new understanding was apparent in their less guarded, more approachable manner.

The student teacher portrays how by becoming a part of the group, Rose and John were able to relax sufficiently to experience the process rather than intellectualise about it. They seemed to bring to the group a feeling that the group as mother could be overwhelming and that their survival depended on keeping a distance. Their defences weren't attacked but with acceptance they were able to merge with its Matrix and yet retain their individuality. It is easy to collude with the wish to retain the adult, functioning, verbal self that group members invariably bring and feel safe with. When Rose and John (or others) confront me or the group, our need is to hold and confirm with a minimum of verbal intervention. It seems to be the feeling of belonging, of relating with other or "the mutative experience which enables change. Hearst (1981) writes:

> Immediate verbal interventions of whatever form are mostly not indicated, even untherapeutic, they repeat and confirm the superior, know-all, contemptuous parental introject.

Foulkes (1946, p. 82) describes this capacity for the group to produce change without focusing on analysis and conscious understanding:

> The most powerful factor in bringing about change is based on ego-training in action and no so much on the insight and the interpretation based on words such as upon corrective action with others.

Idealising

A different example is those people who bring an idealised view and seem to expect a return to merging with the all-compassionate, giving, mother.

Jenny wanted a home birth and seemed to imagine that with her partner, Simon, and her baby they could have an almost ecstatic experience of union. Her pregnancy appeared to have been easy, or they hadn't allowed themselves or anyone else to know about the difficulties. She presented in a glow, an aura of self-satisfaction and pleasure. Simon is attentive and they talk of the water pool they have hired and the many preparations they have made for their natural birth. This has been despite parental antagonism and financial difficulties that they gloss over. There is no apparent anxiety about the birth nor the baby who, they anticipate will be born in water, sleep in their bed, feed on demand and, therefore, be contented and happy.

Again, in this situation, there is the importance of trusting and valuing the group in its capacity to enable this couple to feel heard and accepted but also to allow and modify their idealism and do the necessary worrying. Menzies (1961) describes Janis's idea of the work of worrying

the effects of anticipated traumatic events can be alleviated if an advance opportunity is provided to work over the anxieties

He sees this as a parallel to Freud's concept of the "period of mourning".

THE MEANING OF PAIN

A discussion on pain can be useful for Simon, Jenny and the group. There are bound to be differences on this topic and if they are not expressed I will invite their expression. As Foulkes (1946) says, the group analyst will "promote tolerance and appreciation of individual differences". There are likely to be group members who anticipate horrendous pain and others who imagine pain can be avoided, with many in between.

I ask them to consider their feelings about pain in labour. From the start I am suggesting that pain is inevitable. Someone will say that they see little point in unnecessary pain and that it is masochistic to suffer when drugs are available. Someone else will bring in the unreliability of drugs for pain relief, their possible effects on the baby and their wish to experience in full the enormity of what is happening to them. Another person (usually a man) will not see how labour could be such a significant event "it's just an inevitability and nature has got it wrong making it so painful". Maybe a woman disagrees and suggests that he is jealous of women's ability to give birth and all the attention she gets. Another woman may point out that many men push themselves to what she sees as ridiculous levels of endurance in sports. I might bring in that, from my experience, all labours have highs and lows and that even a labour regarded as going very well will have had troughs and times when it felt hard to continue. I often give the example of mountain climbing and how it can be unbearable at times; you feel like giving up, you see false horizons but then you reach the top. You have a sense of achievement and enjoy the view in a way that you wouldn't if you had taken a lift. Someone says that she or he always takes lifts. There is laughter and maybe they are encouraged to consider areas in their lives where they don't "take lifts" by taking the hard route. There is usually a mention of the pressures people feel to have a natural birth and the possibility of a sense of failure if they don't. I may give examples of labours which were satisfying and involved medical intervention and others that seemed unsatisfactory but were natural. I stress that satisfaction comes from feeling the birth as your own achievement in the context of whatever support was needed.

Interchanges like these can create an environment where anxiety is seen as normal; ambivalence may be expressed and different views are accepted. Jenny and Simon contributed little on the subject of pain. Foulkes (1946, p. 33) writes:

> That patients realise other people have similar morbid ideas, anxieties or impulses act as a potent therapeutic agent ... the discussion, interpretation or analysis of such material is, therefore, effective in a number of people at the same tim, even if they merely listen to it.

He calls this a "mirror reaction".

Indeed, this mirroring reaction seemed to help Jenny and Simon who, by the end of the course, had introjected uncertainties. They considered what they would feel like if they had to go to hospital; Jenny talked of her difficulties sleeping because of worries; Simon wondered if he would cope if she got angry with him in labour as he finds her bad moods difficult now.

GOOD ENOUGH LABOUR

Within this containing environment the group gradually offered a realistic view of birth, pregnancy and parenting. This is a modification of the kinds of idealistic, fixed expectations that Jenny and Simon exemplified.

It could be that we are aiming for the idea of the "good enough labour". Breen (1992) describes mothers who didn't cope well as those

> who retained an image of good mother as "loving, "patient", "unselfish", "never lost temper" and felt at odds with this image of a perfect selfless mother.

Winnicott's concept of "good enough mother" is common currency but whether it is internalised or not depends on the opportunity to work it through, test it out and share. Price (1988, p. 141) says that:

> the women who survive the trauma of disillusionment with the social experience of mothering are those who have close, non-critical relationships with other women.

This is the atmosphere which can be created in the group as regards childbirth as well as mothering and the two are inextricably linked.

PRACTISING MOTHERING IN THE GROUP

Shock of the New

An article in the Guardian (1992) "The Shock of the New" bemoans the fact that prospective parents are ill-prepared for life with a new baby. Bailey writes:

> Pregnant women, it seems, have a block about the final outcome of their state. There is so much emphasis on having a positive birth experience that there is a tendency to forget what is much more important—preparation for the baby.

She says parents themselves complain that they "weren't told" and an Active Birth teacher is quoted as saying: "I tell them until I am blue in the face to prepare for afterwards but they seem to find it impossible to see beyond the birth".

Group analysts know that "ramming home methods" aren't helpful. I have, so far, given two examples of the kinds of pre-verbal experiences, of mirroring, modelling and of belonging to a matrix that enables people to be open to change. I want to develop this idea that by practising mothering in the group "the shock of the new" can be lessened.

Experiencing Physical Care

I have already mentioned that the groups involve physical contact; women with women in yoga, with their partners in partners' groups. People connect through touch, holding and breathing as well as gaining a sense of each other's rhythms. As a basis for this, women are encouraged to learn about their bodies and their physical needs through yoga where they can stretch and develop their strength. This physical side of things is a direct link with the labouring woman and baby, both of whose survival, at the least, lies in their physical care.

During such physical practice it is possible to draw attention to this shared experience so when they may be working together in pairs, breathing, touching, moving and so on, I will talk of the contact they are making which is non-verbal. I suggest that they feel looked after and supported through the attention to each other's needs and rhythms. I point out that the care they get now can be compared to that which they will give their infants. Whilst practising positions for labour I make analogies with looking after a small baby; the rocking together that a baby likes but will, as with labour, need variation and change; her need for firm holding that does not display anxiety or tension, as with the baby who is sensitive to a person holding insecurely; her need for a confident but sensitive decision-maker who doesn't give choices when she can't think, such as with a toddler who has a tantrum if choices are given at the wrong moment.

The group contribute their own ideas; using the breathing and noises to comfort a small baby; the concept "kind but firm" for the support required; the constant quiet and affirmative talk that they get from me in practice, for use in labour and with their infants.

However, I maintain that it is not only the connections made now that have words put to them, which are significant. It is the physical and emotional experiences themselves of receiving and giving care, which can be internalised.

ACTING OUT IN THE GROUP

Psychosomatic "Solutions"

I want to consider some other "here and now" issues which arise and provide an opportunity for exchange and understanding. Sometimes group members will have physical symptoms which make it hard to participate, such as back ache or stiffness. These may be women who have found a psychosomatic solution to psychic pain "repeating their infantile experience of a mother who can care for the body but not the feelings" (Pines, 1980). These will be attended to, but not emphasised as an obstacle and the group will be trusted to do the holding (in the ways I have described). Some women may later project their suffering onto their babies who will then have continual symptoms. The post-natal group provides an opportunity for sharing these as well as containment. Garland's idea (1992) of the "non-problem" is relevant:

> It is precisely through attending to the non-problem that the individual becomes a member of an alternative system to the one in which his symptoms, as an expression of its pathology, was generated and maintained . . . and this process alone, this becoming part of the group (as opposed to attending it) is sufficient to effect change.

Getting It Wrong

Another situation can be where a partner is "getting it wrong" and the woman feels critical and unsure of his capacity to "mother" her both now, in labour and later with the baby. Price (1988, p. 101) writes:

Many women feel disillusioned with her partner's responses to their increased needs, it may be the first time that her needs have been larger and more urgent than his.

The group can share each other's anxieties of "not being up to it", the men can express their "pre-squat" nerves (as one man put it) or the arguments because he or she is so hopeless at the massage. There develops an ethos of inevitable conflict between partners, including some humour at the shared struggles, that happen inside and outside the group and will continue to in the labour and also as parents. Arising in the here and now it is brought out into the matrix and group members have an opportunity to play and work with their common concerns.

INEVITABILITY OF SURVIVING

Finally, I want to mention the roll on, roll off, nature of many of the groups which means that people return with their babies to tell the story of their labour and to give an idea of their new lives. This develops a sense that people survive, each experience is legitimate and everyone is valued. It is a model for how they will be treated in their turn. I am impressed at how people remember the details of each other's labours, which is supportive in itself, but also how they are listened to, especially if someone has had a rough time. Hopefully it is because, as Garland (1982) contends:

> It is those who are actively applying themselves to the understanding and clarification of their colleague's problem who are benefiting most from the transaction

Conclusion

In this paper I have developed my idea that the holding required by women during labour is a means of empathising with the holding the infant will ultimately need from her. I have described some of the ways that groups, which are an application of Group Analysis, can be used for women and men in the child-bearing year with illustrations from my work. I feel that it is important to add that this need for holding continues postnatally and that on-going groups with babies provide a significant "holding experience" which build on the earlier phases and continue to ameliorate and work with "the Shock of the New".

To conclude, I feel it is important to comment on the position of the group conductor or teacher as the person who provides the model for the holding. In this role it is important to be able to carry or hold the projective identifications, not to act on them, neither by becoming the idealised "earth mother", nor the critical, threatened or frightened mother. The conductor's potential for acting out her countertransference is, as always, there. She needs to understand and trust her own feelings and those lived out in the group. She merely assists in the ordinary care that the group provides, that is ultimately internalised without thinking. The omnipotent mother figure has no place but is a real danger given the nature of the work and the client's dependency needs. The most important role of the conductor is to be able to allow and trust the group process. My own capacity to do this must, amongst other things, relate to my own experiences of being a baby, my own early mothering, my own labours, being a mother of a small baby and belonging to groups at these times myself. These represent both the most painful and satisfying holding experiences of my life and I feel privileged to be able to be involved with women, men, babies and groups at this time.

REFERENCES

Bailey, R. (1992). *The Shock of the New*. London. Guardian Newspaper.

Breen, D. (1985). *The Experience of Having a Baby*. London, Free Association.

Davis, M. and Wallbridge, D. (1981) *Boundary and Space: An Introduction to the work of D.W. Winnicott*. London, Karnac.

Ernst, S. and Maguire, M. (1987). *Living with the Sphinx*. London, Women's Press.

Foulkes, S.H. (1946). *Therapeutic Group Analysis*. London, Allen and Unwin.

Garland, C. (1982). *Taking the Non-Problem Seriously*. Group Analysis.

Glenn, L. (1987). *Attachment Theory and Group Analysis*. Group Analysis.

Hearst, L. (1981). *The Emergence of the Mother in the Group*. Group Analysis.

Kitzinger, S. (1992). *Ourselves as Mothers*. London, Doubleday.

Menzies, I. (1961). *The Functioning of Social Systems as a Defence against Anxiety*. London, Tavistock.

Murray, L. (1989). *Winnicott and the Developmental Psychology of Infancy*. British Journal of Psychotherapy.

Nitsun, M. (1989). *Early Development and the Group*. Group Analysis.

Orbach, S. (1993). *The Art of Give and Take*. London, Guardian Newspaper.

Phillips, A. (1985). *Winnicott*. London, Fontana Modern Masters.

Pines, D. (1972). *Pregnancy and Motherhood*. British Journal of Medical Psychology.

Pines, D. (1980). *Skin Communication*. International Journal of Psychoanalysis.

Price, J. (1988). *Motherhood, What it does to your Mind*. London, Pandora.

Prodgers, A. (1990). *The Dual Nature of the Group as Mother: the Uroboric Container*. Group Analysis.

Raphael-Leff, J. (1991). *Psychological Processes of Child-bearing*. London, Chapman and Hall.

Roberts, J. (1982). *Foulkes Concept of the Matrix*. Group Analysis.

Scheidlinger, S. (1974). *On the Concept of the "Mother Group"*. International Journal for Group Psychotherapy.

Skynner, R. (1983). *Families and How to Survive Them*. London, Methuen.

Van der Kleij (1974). *About the Matrix*. Group Analysis.

Winnicott, D.W. (1947). *Further Thoughts on Babies. In: The Child, the Family and the Outside World*. London, Penguin 1964.

Winnicott, D.W. (1958). *Through Paediatrics to Psychoanalysis*. London, Hogarth.

Winnicott, D.W. (1987). *Babies and their Mothers*. U.S.A., Addison-Wesley.

Winterton (1992). *Report into Maternity Services*. London, HMSO.

Wright, K. (1991). *Vision and Separation*. London, Free Association.

LULLABIES AND RHYMES IN THE EMOTIONAL LIFE OF CHILDREN AND NO LONGER CHILDREN

Renata De Benedetti Gaddini

This paper was given as a Squiggle Foundation Public Lecture in December 1993.

Falling asleep, in psychological terms, means losing control of reality and plunging into a world of fantasy.

This moment does not seem to be as meaningful to the vigilant and aware adult, whose external and internal realities are two distinct and unmistakable territories, as it is, instead, to the child in his first years of life. No anxiety can be compared in intensity and duration to the anguish experienced by an infant when he shuts his eyes and consequently loses control of external reality, which is objective, shared and constant, and, to some extent predictable: when the infant is alone in the unpredictable world of his own internal reality where ruthless fantasies take place, he often struggles to maintain contact with a reassuring external reality. In the first years of life, the way in which various children face this experience is strictly connected to the vicissitudes they have encountered while relating to the primal object and to their fear of losing it: in other words, this has to do with the originary mother-child relationship.

Since this phenomenon constitutes one of the most important events of infancy, it becomes essential to a comprehensive study of the early years. The baby seeks reunion with mother in order to alleviate the fears and anxiety caused by the experience of separation when he is forced to relinquish the constancy of objective reality.

In his eyes, this reunion with mother embodies all the qualities and protective prerogatives that could reassure him and allay his fears. But how does the normal infant achieve this reunion with mother after having experienced separation from her? One of the more common methods used by small children is to adopt an object that soon becomes indispensable for him (or her) and appears to be a valuable mother substitute. This could be a piece of blanket or sheet, a cushion or teddy-bear. In due time the substitute assumes the value of an intermediate object between the infant and the outside world and is extremely important for him/her, not only at bed time but also whenever he feels lonely, sad and depressed—a true talisman—whose function may last well into puberty or, sometimes, even into adulthood. Many mothers intuitively recognize the importance of their baby's "possession" and keep this object handy for moments of tension, avoiding even washing it so as not to modify its global sensory configuration, since they fear any change that could alter its value for the infant. Winnicott, who was the first to grasp the profound significance that this object has for the small child, coined the term "transitional" inasmuch as it originates in an intermediate area—between external and internal reality—where the infant is fused with mother and, therefore, protected and secure (Winnicott, 1953).

Since 1953, Winnicott's interpretation of these objects within the infant's psychic reality has become classic and proof to corroborate his theory is constantly growing. Nevertheless, one must regretfully note that systematic studies of transitional phenomena have been relatively few and much too often the use of the term has become imprecise.

According to Winnicott's views, the infant in search of comfort overlaps communications between subjective and shared reality, which can then be perceived objectively. Winnicott indicates this intermediate space (where the overlapping occurs), perceived objectively, as the transitional area. Elements of self as well as of those of the surrounding world are to be found in this space.

By symbolizing the protective reunion with mother in an object, the normal infant discovers and invents a healthy fashion of facing the anxiety of separation.

Not all infants, however, acquire the capacity to create a transitional object or a transitional phenomenon. One may well ask: what do other children—the ones who do not symbolize protective reunion with mother in an object or phenomenon—do when they fall asleep? How can they fend off the terrifying subjective reality that attains to the state of sleep and how do they break off from the reassuring constancy of the objective world that belongs to the state of wakefulness?

ROCKING

As an alternative to the transitional object, in Western culture one frequently finds the habit of rocking infants in arms or in the cradle, sometimes accompanying the child's descent into slumber with a lullaby or a nursery rhyme or a prayer.

The child's imploration for comfort while separating from the outside world is implicit in all of these ways of helping him to fall asleep. In the absence of a transitional object, which through sensory reminiscence symbolized reunion with mother, the infant is afraid of abandoning shared reality and his control over it. Thus, the infant seeks comfort in being rocked either by maintaining direct contact with mother's body or a mother-substitute, such as being rocked in someone's arms until he falls asleep or, in developing countries, the child simply goes to sleep while being carried on his mother's back. This reunion can take place in a less concrete fashion, without physical contact, by means of a lullaby or the crooning of nonsense verse, where the rhymes, with their verbal structure based on an effective non-rational code (Fonari would say "maternal code"), promote a reassuring return to the protective fusion of earliest infancy (Faber, 1988).

But does rocking an infant in one's arms, or putting him/her to sleep on the mother's back to the rhythm of her movements in contact with her body have the same value as an inanimate object which establishes a bridge between me and not-me, between internal and external reality as is proper to the transitional object? As we know, by definition, the transitional object, besides being inanimate, is distinct and separate from the mother's body as well as from the infant; it is a first attempt to establish a relation with the outside world as distinct and separate from self.

Being rocked in mother's arms, while keeping close physical contact with her, renders external reality a bit less strange and at the same time helps it maintain the primitive and concrete character that is typical of precursors (pre-objects, still Me, *not* a bridge between Me and not-Me). (1)

It is probable that a lullaby sung in the cradle or in the bed lies halfway between a transitional object and being rocked in the arms, and to a certain extent, embodies a symbolization of the lost reunion that is intrinsic to the transitional object. During the rocking of an infant in the cradle to the sound of a lullaby or a nursery rhyme or nonsense rhymes (Orengo N., 1972), the rhythms, cadences and above all the rhymes and phonic games help the infant re-experience the reassuring fusion he had lost and, consequently, empower him to control his relationship with external reality by modulating separation.

In couplets or alternate rhymes, as in the rhythmic singing of lullabies that alternate fusionality and separation, and closely follow the vocalizing and inner rhythms of the sleepy infant, one can gain insight into how the concepts of time and space of being-at-one and separate are formed and how all this facilitates the process of individuation.

THE GENESIS OF TRANSITIONAL OBJECTS
AND TRANSITIONAL PHENOMENA

According to the theory of transitional objects and transitional phenomena (T.O. and T.P.) four fundamental ingredients seem to lie at the base of the infant's capacity to form early symbols:

(1) The infant must have had a mother that was "good-enough" (the term is Winnicott's and implies the *relativity* of this characteristic to the needs of a particular infant) to earn the child's trust and make him desire to maintain his protective reunion with her: this means he must have had a good early objectual relationship. The deprived infant, whose mother was not "good-enough" to make him desire to evoke her in objects or phenomena that symbolize reunion, usually does not have a transitional object nor does he invest it—and for that matter, any object—with affection or particular care.

(2) Given that the infant has succeeded in establishing a relationship of trust with the primary object (the breast), and that he has been able to enjoy the mother's personal good qualities during the day and normally when he goes to bed, it may happen that the infant loses the mother's concrete physical presence; this determines a certain dose of frustration which gives way to anxiety. In other words, the mother must be "good-enough" to motivate the infant's desire for continuous contact, but must also be sufficiently sure of herself to be capable of permitting him to face the process of individuation on his own.

(3) It is important that the infant experiences frustration and the fear of physically losing his mother (that is, of not having her continued reassuring presence) in a critical period when his imagination begins to exist in a consistent and organized fashion, approximately between 8 months and the end of the second year of life.

(4) The infant must possess an object capable of symbolizing his reunion with mother belonging to the period of the earliest care experienced as a part of the mother, and—as such—invested with trust. (2)

In fact, at the time of our research, this fourth point did not seem as important to us as the former three. First of all, the blanket, sought by the infant before falling asleep is a representation of the coverlet mother wrapped him up in when he was nursed and similarly the nylon or linen the baby loves to fondle is, in fact, a reminiscence of mother's blouse or nightgown that had perhaps caressed the infant's cheek while he suckled at her breast. These are cutaneous perceptions experienced during the period of fusion at the breast that the child tries to evoke at a later moment, even in absence of the woollen blanket or while attempting to re-experience protected fusion and reunion. As proof of this hypothesis we have statistics that indicate how children who are born in autumn and winter use woollen or furry objects more frequently than children born in spring and summer who generally prefer objects made of nylon or linen (fig.l); this proves that the absence of a specific object cannot be adduced as a cause of the non-invention of a transitional object. (3)

LULLABIES

Apart from transitional objects, lullabies, nonsense and nursery rhymes and other phonic games are used to put infants to sleep (transitional phenomena = T.P.). Among the many, I should like to recall a particular lullaby sung by a Calabrian grandmother while rocking her year-old grandchild to sleep. The song was almost a dirge and I was not so interested in its verbal content and the meaning of the words (almost incomprehensible) as in the way the woman accompanied it with cadenced vocalisms resembling a litany more than a song to put a baby to sleep. In this way she actively adapted herself to the infant's need of wakeful-ness and sleep, presence and absence.

"dormi e riposa
lu bellow della mamma . . .
vedo il sigillo del mio cuore
dormi, bambino, fai la nanna"

"sleep and rest
mama's darling . . .
I see the seal of my heart.
Sleep, baby, hush-a-bye".

In this dirge, full of arabesque-like vocalisms, it is easy to perceive the grandmother's capacity to identify herself with the sleepy baby and respond to his needs. The rhythm, created by the beating of the cradle rocking against the floor, gradually slows down as the infant stops crying but immediately accelerates and the grandmother raises her voice when the child resumes whimpering, coming to a halt only when he definitively

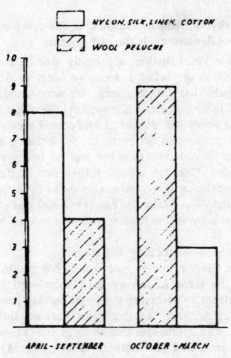

Figure 1

falls asleep. This is one of the most astonishing examples of what Winnicott meant when speaking of "good-enough" mothers, capable of actively adapting to their child's needs. (4)

One can appreciate four aspects of the complex structure underlying this lullaby and its rhythms:

(1) The rhythms determined by the beating of the rocking-chair on the floor during the first part of the lullaby. In the recording, we counted 33 beats per minute during the first two minutes; in these two minutes the infant gradually passes from crying to sleep. At this point the rhythmic beat of the rocking-chair slows down to 27 beats a minute for the following two minutes. It then accelerates irregularly to 32 beats, then down to 30 and finally peters out until the rocking ceases all together.

(2)   The rocking rhythm lasts ten minutes, the entire duration of the lullaby.

(3)   The vocal rhythm, whose intensity in this complex mixture of human rhythms diminishes, is the last to cease.

(4)   The pauses in vocal rhythm, apparently used by the grandmother to adapt herself to the infant's needs in order to determine, for example, if baby has fallen asleep, are accompanied by a gradual lowering of her voice; but if she realized that the infant is not asleep yet and still needs her, she sings louder and accelerates the rhythm until she is certain that her presence, symbolizing an archaic fusion with mother in order to face the fear of being abandoned, is no longer needed. One can almost follow her in the vicissitudes of empathic vocalisms: the grandmother rocks the baby and sings. The infant is quiet. She thinks she can leave him and stops rocking and singing. The baby still needs her presence and we hear him wine.

The grandmother resumes rocking and singing.

The lyrics of a German lullaby recorded by Margarete von Trotta seem concerned with the sense of having been abandoned felt by an infant before going to sleep; by reversing the situation they pretend that it is the mother who is abandoned: "Mother cries because little Johann is no longer with her". Von Trotta said that when at age two or three she heard this lullaby she reassured her mother: "Don't cry, Mamma, I'll never leave you". In this context, she recalled her childhood during World War II and how at a very early age she had perceived the insecurity felt by the adults in her entourage, who were witnesses to the daily collapse of surrounding buildings and continually exposed to separation, destruction and death.

RHYMES AND PLAYING WITH WORDS

In his volume on jokes, Freud (1905) draws our attention to the fact that phonic games, where vowels and consonants are repeated in rhymes, cause pleasure and are cognate to the earliest babbling of infants.

Holland (1968), in acknowledging Freud's apt comparison, links it to other sources of gratification: among these, reassurance. But what kind of reassurance can be evoked by rhymes and word games? The rhyme unites two sounds, i.e. two different elements (Novarino, 1992). There is, therefore, a reunion after separation, which is the basic element of all transitional objects and transitional phenomena. And this is the reassurance the infant seeks as he falls asleep and that gratifies him when mother sings a lullaby.

DEEP EMOTIONAL STATES

Although the first decades of psychoanalysis had the great merit of shedding light on the formation of mind and emotional life, there is still much to learn about the process of formation that permits symbols, affects and thoughts to emerge and assume a mental form on the basis of (physical) concrete sensations which have been experienced within the ambit of the first interactions with mother.

It was the English school of psychoanalysis (Fairbairn, Winnicott, et al.) that introduced the theory of object-relation, oriented towards these first interactions, in place of the earlier theory of instincts. The latter was based on Freud's original concept that the newborn possesses potent instincts and "drives", which, when repressed in their encounter with civilization and culture, constitute the basis of all psychotherapy. The object-relation theory derives from Melanie Klein's discoveries of the nature of the small child's emotional life and origin of his unconscious fantasies, where the earliest mother-infant interactions are of pre-eminent interest.

Within the ambit of these theoretical views and particularly in their formulation by Winnicott, (1971, pp.12-14) the "good-enough" mother(s) starts out by adapting herself almost completely to the infant's needs. As time passes, little by little this mother perceives that her child's needs diminish as he acquires reassurance and emotional growth, and she will tend to withdraw her "active adaptation" to begin relating sensibly and continuously to the child's capacity, based on previous experience, of accepting the fact that mother can leave him sporadically and no longer be at his total disposal every minute of the day and night. Then the infant will have overcome the state of absolute dependence where only needs existed and reached a state of relative dependence, where his needs can wait, leaving space for desire. Only at this point can the infant experience frustration at a level that is completely different from a situation of dire necessity.

THE PLEASURE OF RHYMES

The pleasure the infant finds in the rhymes of lullabies and nonsense verse originates, therefore, in the fusional area of earliest life and has the capacity of filling the void created by separation. Being at-one becomes being at-two, a couple that is anchored to phonic unity.

When we are adults, our emotional participation in this ritual made of rhymes and assonances has to do with our re-living the reassurance we have gained from cultural experience and that gives us the possibility of recovering the illusory and paradoxical aspects of life in phonic play—a life that proceeds continuously through states of internalized separation and fusion. For example, I recently observed an expression of attentive hilarity and pleasure on the faces of some youngsters who were listening to Toti Scialoia's nonsense rhymes. Here is one:

"L'ape che fuma pepe
lo preme nella pipa
lo aspira come un papa
lo sputa cupa cupa
oltre le siepi in fior."

(The bumble bee smokes pepper
and presses it in the pipe
and inhales it like a pope
and spits it out out, out
beyond the flowering hedge).

and another:

"Di notte quando i gatti sono spenti
ho scritto pochi versi, quasi lenti.
Di giorno, quando i gatti sono attenti
ho fritto molti vermi, quasi venti."

(At night when cats go out
I wrote some lines in doubt.
In the daytime, when cats are plenty
I fried lots of worms, almost twenty).

RHYMES AND LULLABIES
IN THE PROCESS OF SEPARATION-INDIVIDUATION

Rhymes and lullabies can, therefore, be seen as a "game" that takes place in the area where the original parameters of differentiation and the entire process of separation-individuation are established. The reassuring function of rhyme is cognate to that of rhythm, which, although more primitive, articulates the structuring elements. In fact, rhythm, more than rhyme, comes closer to the biological basis of being, and has been universally acknowledged as the natural tranquillizer that from the time immemorial calms children by repeating sounds and movements.

Rhythm in itself reassures by permitting us to re-evoke the presence of mother, and particularly those sounds and rhythms that are part of her presence, intimately associated with the way we first related to her and that in some way take us back to pre-natal life. Within the context of rhythms, rhymes and phonic play, verbalization can be considered a component of the dynamic configuration that catalyses our return to the time of paradoxes that is a part of psychological birth (Mahler, Pine and Bergman, 1975), a time when fusion and separation live together.

Nursery rhymes offer two or three year-old children an opportunity to repeat and exercise their abilities and play the tortuous game of existence, which at that moment consists in not being able to give up the primary attachment and at the same time wanting to venture out into the realm of separation. (6)

These are elementary operations in the course of personal organization that help to soothe them. Only when the infant can distinguish between perceiving and conceiving (Muensterberger, 1978) will the lullaby cease to be an indispensable companion for falling asleep and assume the identity of a pleasant song, without serving as a transitional phenomenon that is vital to allay fears of separation. Still, for the rest of our lives it will preserve the quality of lying half-way between a pure pleasure principle and a pure reality principle. Its comforting qualities derive precisely from this intermediate position. Even as adults, we cannot forget those magical rhymes with their close assonances and alliterations. Nor can we forget the miracle of those rhymes that continually confirm our capacity to produce doubles, whose single components are fused and distinct at the same time ("Memory and hope", Stedman, N.D., 'The Nature and Elements of Poetry', quoted in Faber 1988).

I find Faber's (1988) remarks very apt about poetry as such facing inwards as well as outwards and leading up to a metaphor where identity and difference can be objectivized.

Lullabies and nursery rhymes contain traces of this primal poetic element, and for this reason have the capacity to reassure the sleepy child who, as an adult, will find joy and comfort in music or poetry.

NOTES

(1) During a vast study (in 1968) conducted in collaboration with Winnicott over a period of five years and in three distinct social groups, we called precursors those objects that have the capacity to comfort an infant in a unique, irreplaceable manner, but which are neither discovered nor invented by him—rather they are either presented by the mother or are parts of the infant's or the mother's body precursors (of transitional objects). Besides the thumb and fingers which are part of play and hand-mouth exploration typical of 4-8

month-old infants, we also considered precursors certain traditional objects such as the dummy/pacifier or the rubber nipple used as a pacifier, or the tongue, the lips, the wrist or the back of the hand, the mother's or baby's hair or the ears, nose, mouth or a mole, all of which are touched or smoothed in the intent of receiving a tactile sensation associated with sucking or other combined actions. What usually happens with the pacifier is that the mother shoves it into the infant's mouth so that he has no alternative except to be tranquillized. "What is so completely absent in the pacifier technique is the baby's reaching out toward . . . in other words, there is no allowance for the baby's creative capacity which shows in the way, for instance, that the hand may reach towards an object, or the mouth itself which may go towards an object in terms of saliva" (Winnicott, 1965). Sometimes, we hesitated about whether to classify a mother's or a grandmother's hand, ear, hair, or any other cutaneous appendix, such as a mole (which after some time can be substituted by the infant's own bodily appendices) as precursors, or as true transitional objects. In fact, these objects seem to have the exclusive protective value of a talisman, typical of transitional objects. Still Winnicott is explicit when he writes of the latter: "It is lucky that the child uses this object (transitional object) and not the mother herself or the lobe of her ear or her hair" (Winnicott, 1965). The characteristics of transitional objects should, therefore, comprise these elements: they must be outside the mother's and the infant's body; they must be discovered or invented by the infant who symbolically attempts to evoke a reunion with mother from when he has experienced separation; they must have been discovered or invented when the infant's imaginative capacity began to develop; they must have the unique capacity of consoling the child in situations of tension and fear like those experienced when falling asleep. Bearing these concepts in mind, we did not regard as transitional objects any of these cutaneous appendices, whether of the mother or of the infant himself, even if they possessed several of the above-mentioned prerogatives. (i.e. being discovered by the child or having the unique capacity to console him in a moment of fear). We did not define them as such because they are not symbolic but rather a part of the mother's real body. In many cases we were able to distinguish that a mother's symbiotic bond (for example a depressed mother who fears losing her tie with the child and remaining alone) is the factor that hinders the infant in his attempt to symbolize his reunion with her. This is what happens in the case of her physical presence in the same bed or in the same room; in these cases, one rarely finds that the infant has "invented" a transitional object.

This second group of logical assumptions has led to the formulation of the following working hypotheses:

- The presence of transitional objects is inverse to the quantity of precursors.
- The presence of precursors depends on the type of relationship existing between the partial object (the breast) and the infant in terms of mode of nursing (fixed time or demand feeding) and the eventual proffering or non-proffering of a pacifier.

• The manner of putting the child to sleep in early infancy *may not only influence his capacity to play imaginatively* and to relate to others but also at a *cognitive level, his future capacity of symbolization and abstraction and, at an emotional level, his capacity to believe in and trust and commit himself to the things in which he believes.*

(2) In a restricted environment, child-care personnel in orphanages ascribe the lack of these objects, repeatedly observed in committed children, to the fact that there exists no material with which they can create them. The missing relationship of trust renders the affectionate investment of an object impossible.

(3) Prior to this research, a corollary to these considerations had been the observation of how Italian children are usually put to bed with the sheets and covers accurately tucked in while in other cultures, for example in Anglo-Saxon countries, sheets and covers are simply laid over the infant, almost as if they were left for the child to discover. This observation is particularly apt in the case of the rural group but it seems extendable to numerous Mediterranean populations and to Latin peoples in general, apart from other ethnic and social groups in developing countries. Because these various ways of covering children in bed concern our rural group above all and are related to the almost authoritarian mode in which those mothers often manipulate their infants, as if they were almost an extension of themselves, it is legitimate to think that this has influenced their capacity to "invent" a transitional object.

(4) Winnicott showed great interest in this lullaby that adapted itself so aptly to the child's needs as it fell asleep. Unfortunately he did not see the work which was published in 1970 (Gaddini R. & E. 1970) where ample reference was made to it.

(5) Winnicott never speaks of a good mother but of a "good-enough" one which refers to the needs of the particular child who is her infant. A "good-enough mother" therefore is not an absolute concept but a relative one.

(6) The infant Jesus's hand on the Virgin Mary's breast while the other is on a pear offered him by an angel, that we note in Correggio's "La madonna del latte", as seen by Goethe (1787) and that many have admired as "The weaning of Christ", seems to me an excellent illustration of this paradoxical moment of development when the child on the one hand wishes to continue being at-one with mother and at the same time seeks separation.

REFERENCES

Faber, M.D. (1988) The Pleasures of Rhymes: a Psychoanalytic Note. *International Review of Psychoanalysis* 15. 375.

Freud, S. (1905) *Jokes and their Relation to the Unconscious*. Standard Edition 8.

Gaddini E., & Gaddini, R. (1970) Transitional Objects and the Process of Individuation: a Study in Three Different Social Groups. *Journal of the*

American Academy of Child Psychiatry 9.2. pp347-365. In Gaddini E., "*Scritti* (1953-85)" Ed. Cortina 1989 and in English in Gaddini E., " *A Psychoanalytical Theory of Infantile Experience*". Routledge, London/New York 1992.

Gaddini, R. (1986) I precursori degli oggetti e dei fenomeni transizionali. Rivista di Psicoanalisi. 2. 281-295.

Gaddini, R. (1987) "Early Care and the Roots of Internalization". International Review of Psychoanalysis. 14-321.

Holland, N. (1968) *The Dynamics of Literary Response.* New York/Oxford (quoted by Faber)

Mahler, M., Pine, F., Bergman, A. (1975) *The Psychological Birth of the Human Infant.* Basic Books: New York.

Muensterberger, W. (1978) "Between Reality and Fantasy" In *Between Reality and Fantasy.* Edited by Grolnick S., and Barkin. Aronson Publications. New York.

Nissim Momigliano, L. (1991) "Il the nel deserto" Rivista di Psicoanalisi 4. p.799.

Novarino, D. (1992) Personal communication.

Orengo, N. (1972) *A-Uli-uli Filastrocche, Conte e Ninna-nanna.* Einaudi Ed.

Winnicott, D.W. (1953) Transitional Objects and Transitional Phenomena, in *Through Paediatrics to Psychoanalysis,* London: Hogarth Press, 1978.

Winnicott, D.W. (1965) Unpublished letters to Renata Gaddini.

Winnicott, D.W. (1971) *Playing and Reality.* Tavistock Publications pp. 12-14.

A HISTORICAL ANALYSIS OF WINNICOTT'S "THE USE OF AN OBJECT"

Laurel Samuels, Ph.D.

SUMMARY

"The Use of an Object" was Winnicott's last major work. Since its original presentation in 1968 it has come to be regarded as one of his most important contributions to psychoanalysis but also as one of his most enigmatic. The goal of this discussion is to reconsider the paper by examining it in historical context, including the original version, discussion, and unpublished correspondence. The concept of object usage was separated from its historical context, thereby subtly altering its meaning. An exploration of the relationship between object usage, play and transitional phenomena allows another vantage point from which to view Winnicott's unique contribution.

On 12 November 1968, Winnicott presented his last major paper, "The Use of an Object", to the New York Psychoanalytical Society. The paper is regarded not only as one of his most important contributions to psychoanalysis but also as one of his most enigmatic. It has provided a powerful concept for understanding the earliest phases of human development and has led to new explanations of the symbols of Christian theology (Grotstein, 1994; Hopkins, 1989). Yet in comparison with other Winnicottian concepts such as the transitional object or the holding environment, the concept of object usage remains elusive and difficult to apply.[1]

In this discussion I would like to reconsider the paper by looking at it in historical context. I will cite material from three sources: (1) the original paper and unpublished discussion from the New York Psychoanalytic Institute, (2) letters in the Winnicott archives, and (3) Winnicott's posthumously published papers. I will argue that the concept of object usage was separated from its historical context, thereby subtly altering its meaning. I will explore the relationship between object usage, play and transitional phenomena with the hope that this will allow another vantage point from which to view Winnicott's unique contribution.

THEMES IN "THE USE OF AN OBJECT"

Theory of Interpretation

The paper can be conceptualized as having four interwoven themes. The first is Winnicott's theory of interpretation, a statement of his increasing awareness of the need to wait for the patient to arrive at understanding. This theme originated in his work as early as "The Observation of Infants in a Set Situation" (Davis, 1993b). He describes a group of patients, whom he calls borderline cases, who cannot yet use interpretation. He writes, "It appalls me to think how much change I have prevented or delayed in patients *in a certain classificatory category* by my personal need to interpret. If only we can wait the patient arrives at understanding creatively and with immense joy, and I now enjoy this joy more than I used to enjoy the sense of having been clever" (Winnicott, 1969). For these patients, change will depend less upon interpretive work than upon the analyst's survival.

Introduction of the Term "Object Usage"

The second theme is Winnicott's introduction of the term object usage. He has selected a term that heretofore would have implied exploitation to describe a more advanced stage of relating, one in which the object's separate existence must be taken into consideration. His choice of terminology is paradoxical and even has a certain shock value, as does his well known aphorism "There is no such thing as a baby." He playfully contrasts meanings of the word: For the object to be "used", it must be "used". While the term has now made its way into the psychoanalytic literature, it could be argued that it stands between the reader and understanding. Certainly it was a red flag for the discussants at the original presentation.

Meaning of the Term "Object Usage"

The third theme, the core of Winnicott's contribution, is his statement of the meaning of object usage. This is Winnicott's reformulation of the depressive position as first outlined by Klein (1935,1940). Winnicott had addressed this subject in a series of papers throughout his long career: "The Manic Defense" (1935), "The Depressive Position in Normal Emotional Development" (1954), "Psychoanalysis and the Sense of Guilt"

(1958), and "The Development of the Capacity for Concern" (1963). In "The Use of an Object" Winnicott reaffirms his belief in the crucial importance of the environment. The capacity to use an object, he writes, is another example of a maturational process that depends upon a facilitating environment. Here Winnicott emphasizes the importance of the mother's actual ability to survive the infant's attacks without retaliation. He no longer mentions the role of the reparative gesture as he did in his earlier writings. This is the most radical revision proposed in the paper and one that was not grasped by the discussants. Later interpreters (Newman, 1989; Ogden, 1986, 1989, 1994; Phillips, 1988; Rudnytsky, 1991) will see this as the heart of Winnicott's contribution and as an acknowledgement of his divergence from Klein. Phillips put the matter succinctly:

> . . . So for Winnicott, Klein's concept of the depressive position now seemed more like a protection racket, a sophisticated version of being nice to mother. In Winnicott's view, the object was not reconstituted by the subject's reparation—as Klein believed—but constituted by its own survival (Phillips, 1988, p. 132).

Theory of Aggression

The fourth theme is Winnicott's theory of aggression. He is asking for no less than a revision of drive theory. He is describing an impulse to destroy that becomes destructive only if the object fails to survive. Whereas in classical theory reality is attacked because it frustrates, Winnicott is suggesting that destruction (with survival) creates reality by placing the object outside the area of omnipotent control. This is one of the most controversial aspects of the paper as well as one of the most misunderstood.

HISTORICAL CONTEXT

The original version of the paper (and, with some modifications, the version published in the 1969 *International Journal of Psychoanalysis*) contains several paragraphs deleted when the paper was revised. This deleted material gives a different vantage point on the concept of object usage. Winnicott begins the paper by stating that the idea of the use of an object grows out of his work on the transitional object and is related to the capacity to play.[2]

> This work on the use of an object arises out of my clinical experience and is in the direct line of development that is peculiarly mine. . . My work on transitional objects and phenomena which followed naturally on after

"The Observation of Infants in a Set Situation" is fairly well know, largely because of Miss Freud's generous reference to this work. Obviously the idea of the use of an object is related to the capacity to play... All this makes sense, for me, of the special focus that there is in my work on what I have called transitional phenomena and the study of the minute details that illustrate the gradual build up of the individual's capacity to find and then to use the "external world" with its own independence and autonomy (Winnicott, 1969).

This paragraph was deleted when the paper was published in *Playing and Reality*, the most widely cited version of "The Use of an Object". I would like to suggest that the effect of this revision was to separate the concept from its historical context and subtly alter its meaning. I will return to this point after describing the history of the paper.

In October 1968, in preparation for his trip to New York, Winnicott sent a copy of his paper to Anna Freud. As quoted above, he had made reference to her role in the acceptance of his concept of the transitional object. Miss Freud replied:[3]

> 20 Maresfield Gardens
> London, N.W.3
> October 30, 1968.
>
> Dear Dr. Winnicott,
>
> Thank you very much for sending me the paper which you are going to read to the New York Society. I was very interested to read it and I shall be very interested to know whether you get a good reaction and discussion of it.
>
> As concerns your remark about me, I do not think that our New York colleagues will find this justified. They know your work very well and they will feel that they do not need me to draw their attention to you. I think that your "transitional object" has conquered the analytic world.
>
> Yours sincerely
>
> Anna Freud

There is a hint of a rebuke in her reply, as if she were telling him not to hide behind her skirts. But if Winnicott had doubts about how his paper would be received, his concerns were well founded. Indeed, a question that remains unanswered is why Winnicott chose to present the paper at the New York Psychoanalytic Institute, at that time so hostile to Klein's ideas.

The paper met with misunderstanding and criticism. The discussants for the evening were Edith Jacobson, M.D., Bernard D. Fine, M.D., and Samuel Ritvo, M.D. Unfortunately, their individual discussions, although available for reference, cannot be quoted. The Minutes by David Milrod, M.D., summarize the proceedings well. All quotations are from the minutes.[4]

All of the discussants took up Winnicott's choice of terminology. They strongly objected to his choice of the term "object use" to denote a more advanced stage than object relating. While Jacobson acknowledged that the difference might be one of terminology, she commented that if Winnicott regarded object relating as a process that involved projections and identifications resulting in the depletion of the subject, it was no wonder he needed a new term. Fine agreed and added his own objection to employing a common term of speech to designate a "scientific psychoanalytic process".

Far more controversial was Winnicott's notion of destructive attack and survival. The discussants seemed unfamiliar with the theoretical concepts underlying Winnicott's ideas. As Rudnytsky (1991) has pointed out, the concept of the use of an object is incomprehensible without an understanding of its Kleinian underpinning. Jacobson is quoted as saying that she could not understand what Winnicott meant by "destructive attack" or "survival" and found extreme his statement that "the object is always being destroyed". Fine noted the absence of any reference to the significance of the libidinal component in helping the object survive. He too did not understand the nature of the destructive process Winnicott was trying to describe.

At the end of the discussion an analyst member of the audience presented a clinical vignette which, perhaps for the sake of argument, almost caricatured Winnicott's concept. Immediately following, Winnicott is quoted as saying that "his concept was torn to pieces and that he would be glad to give it up". It had been a disappointing evening.

Winnicott became ill immediately after the lecture and was admitted to Lenox Hill Hospital. "I was already ill," he later wrote to Anna Freud (Rodman, 1987). He was hospitalized for five weeks, several in the Intensive Cardiac Care Unit. He and Mrs. Winnicott, who had accompanied him to New York, were unable to return to London until 20 December 1968. Winnicott's correspondence from this time period is about his illness. Colleagues and friends from around the world sent wishes for his recovery. Now 72, Winnicott had a history of coronary disease and knew the seriousness of his illness. Ever the natural scientist, he observed his own reactions and spoke of writing about his experiences as a patient. One of his chief concerns was to be his hospital bill, which came to a staggering $3,561.

Along with their concerns about his health, Winnicott's correspondents expressed regrets about the reception his paper had received. Masud Khan (27 November 1968) wrote:[5]

I do not think one can use the concept "failure" regarding your paper in New York. Of course I don't know how it was received and have been too distressed to write my friends and gather gossip from New York. Of one thing I am sure and that is that the paper on "use of an object" breaks new ground, which of course is always discomfortable for the Pundits in the beginning. I have no doubt that gradually they will take over that concept in America as they did that of the "Transitional object".

A week later (2 December 1968) he wrote a long letter with news from London, and reassuringly added:

I never had any doubt, in spite of your earlier letter, that your paper was a great success in New York and that it has started an intellectual ferment which they will only slowly digest and benefit from.

Several American analysts who had been in the audience wrote to express their indignation. Dr. A wrote, "Edith Jacobson was a lady—but I was rather incensed at the kind of criticism you received from my other analytic colleagues." Dr. B said, "I am still anxious to tell you how deep and lasting an echo your paper left; how unhappy I was about the undeserved response you received."

Winnicott responded to the discussants' criticisms in two short papers, neither of which was published in his lifetime. His editors (Winnicott, Shepherd and Davis, 1989) note that both were unrevised and unedited. Thus the reader has the unusual opportunity to observe how Winnicott went about defending his ideas to his critics. He is still coming to terms with the magnitude of the implications of what he has suggested. The first reply ("Comments on my paper 'The Use of an Object'", 5 December 1968) was written while Winnicott was still in the hospital in New York. He is responding to Fine's criticism that he had overlooked the libidinal components of the drives and their ability to help the object survive. He acknowledges that the main idea of his paper necessitates a major revision of theory. He writes that in health there is a fusion of libidinal and aggressive drives, but "there is a phase prior to that in which the destructive aliveness of the individual is simply a symptom of being alive and has nothing to do with anger at meeting the reality principle" (Winnicott, Shepherd and Davis, 1989, p. 239). Later in the paper, reflecting on what he had just written, he adds, "I see all this may have some flaw in it . . ." (p. 239).

A few months later (16 January 1969) Winnicott returned to the subject in "The Use of an Object in the context of *Moses and Monotheism*". He re-examines the concept of object usage in the context of his lifelong emphasis upon the importance of the environment. He writes, "the drive is potentially destructive, but whether it *is* destructive or not depends on what the object is like; does the object *survive*, that is, does it retain its character, or does it *react*? If the former, then there is no destruction" (Winnicott, Shepherd and Davis, 1989, p. 245).

RELATIONSHIP BETWEEN OBJECT USAGE, PLAY, AND TRANSITIONAL PHENOMENA

Let us now return to the relationship between object usage, play, and transitional phenomena. We have seen how Winnicott's introduction of the concept of object usage met with misunderstanding and criticism. While now regarded as one of Winnicott's most important contributions to psychoanalysis, the concept remains elusive and has not made its way into the literature in the same way as have many of his other ideas. While this undoubtedly has many antecedents, in this paper I have emphasized the role of happenstance and circumstance. The "Use of an Object" is a work in progress. It was Winnicott's last major work, written toward the end of his life, and therefore was not subject to the long period of reworking he gave his other ideas. As a result, the concept is often regarded as if it were separate from the body of his work. Later revisions of the paper, in which several paragraphs relating object usage to play and transitional phenomena were deleted, made this separation of concept from context even more pronounced. The concept suffered what Ogden (1989), in a somewhat different context, calls the collapse of potential space. The idea of object usage was taken literally and lost the sense of paradox that is intrinsic to all Winnicott's work.

How can we interpret Winnicott's statement that the idea of the use of an object is related to transitional phenomena and the capacity to play? I trust that there will be many answers to this question. Let us begin by examining the process by which object usage develops. I would suggest that the object in object usage is neither so different nor the journey to it so long as the decontextualized interpretation would lead us to think. Another way of saying this is that the object "found" in transitional experiencing is also the object that is "used" in object usage. However, the developmental process is not a linear one. There has been a tendency to describe object usage as the most advanced stage in a diachronic developmental sequence, moving from subjectivity to objectivity, from omnipotently created objects through transitional objects to "used" objects. Winnicott does describe the capacity to use an object as a more advanced stage of relating but by no means as radically discontinuous from what preceded it. The process may have both diachronic and synchronic elements (Ogden, 1986) so that object usage develops along with (and not as a development from) transitional phenomena and therefore incorporates qualities of transitional experiencing. This, I believe, is what Eigen refers to when he writes that "the core sense of creativeness that permeates transitional experiencing is *reborn on a new level* in object usage" (Eigen, 1981, p. 415) (italics added).

In closing, I would like to address some of the problems that have arisen as the concept of object usage has been applied to the psychotherapeutic process. As we have seen, Winnicott's concepts of destruction and survival were problematic from the start. There has been a tendency to take literally Winnicott's statement of the need for the analyst to survive the patient's destructive attacks (Slochower, 1994). One is reminded of Jacobson's criticism that Winnicott had "overlooked those psychotic persons who are extremely destructive and whose patient therapists survive the destructive impulses without the positive results he describes" (Milrod, 1968). The resulting interaction seems to be neither use nor "mis-use" (Hamilton, 1991) but rather a malignant object usage that Ghent (1992) calls "ab-use". This would be a very un-Winnicottian notion of psychotherapy.

Once again, Winnicott's statements need to be placed in context. It is helpful to keep in mind one of his other therapeutic maxims: "... *psychotherapy is done in the overlap of the two play areas, that of the patient and that of the therapist. If the therapist cannot play, then he is not suitable for the work. If the patient cannot play, then something needs to be done to enable the patient to become able to play, after which psychotherapy may begin*" (Winnicott, 1971, p. 63). Winnicott reminds us that psychotherapy takes place in the space between two people, the patient and the analyst, and if this space does not exist it must be created before psychotherapy can begin. This gives us a new way to look at the concepts of destruction and survival. The analyst that is being destroyed is both the real analyst and the version of the analyst that is being jointly created in the analytic space. The paradox need not be resolved.

NOTES

I would like to express my gratitude to the colleagues who have generously shared their time and thoughts: Tom Ogden, James Grotstein, John Padel, Earl Hopper and David Millar.

(1) It is beyond the scope of this paper to review all the literature on Winnicott's concept of object usage. A list of major contributes includes: Bollas (1987), Davis (1993 a & b), Eigen (1981), Ghent (1992), Grolnick (1990), Grotstein (1993, 1994), Hamilton (1991), Hopkins (19898), Newman (1987, 1989), Ogden (1986, 1989, 1994), Phillips (1988), Pizer (1992), Rayner (1991), Rudnytsky (1991), Slochower (1994), and Winnicott, Shepherd, & Davis (1989).

(2) Quoted with the permission of the New York Psychoanalytic Institute

and Society.

(3) Courtesy of the Archives of Psychiatry, The New York Hospital–Cornell Medical Center and The Winnicott Trust. Reproduced by permission of Mark Paterson & Associates on behalf of the estate of Anna Freud.

(4) Quoted with the permission of the New York Psychoanalytic Institute and Society.

(5) Courtesy of the Archives of Psychiatry, The New York Hospital–Cornell Medical Center and The Winnicott Trust. Reproduced by permission of Rogers, Coleridge, and White, © Masud Khan 1994.

REFERENCES

Bollas, C. (1987) *The Shadow of the Object: Psychoanalysis of the Unthought Unknown*, London: Free Association.

Davis, M. (1993a) Destruction as an achievement in the work of Winnicott, *Winnicott Studies*, 7: 85–92.

Davis, M. (1993b) Winnicott and the Spatula Game, *Winnicott Studies*, 8: 57–67.

Eigen, M. (1981) The area of faith in Winnicott, Lacan and Bion, *International Journal of Psychoanalysis*, 62: 413–33.

Ghent, E. (1992) Paradox and process, *Psychoanalytic Dialogues*, 2: 135–59.

Grolnick, S. (1990) *The Work and Play of Winnicott*, Northvale, NJ: Jason Aronson.

Grotstein, J. S. (1993) Boundary difficulties in borderline patients. In: B. Boyer & P. Giovacchini (Eds), *Master Clinicians on Treating the Regressed Patient, Vol. 2*, Northvale, NJ: Jason Aronson, 107–41.

Grotstein, J. S. (1994) Projective identification reappraised: Projective identification, introjective identification, the transference / countertransference / neurosis / psychosis, and their consummate expression in the Crucifixion, the Pieta, and therapeutic exorcism. II. The countertransference complex. Unpublished manuscript.

Hamilton, V. (1991) Use or misuse: A clinical illustration of Winnicott's concept of "object usage". Unpublished manuscript.

Hopkins, B. (1989) Jesus and object-use. A Winnicottian account of the resurrection myth, *International Review of Psychoanalysis*, 16, 93–100.

Klein, M. (1935) A contribution to the psychogenesis of manic-depressive states. In: *Love, Guilt and Reparation*, London: Virago.

Klein, M. (1940) Mourning and its relation to manic depressive states. In: *Love, Guilt and Reparation*, London: Virago.

Milrod, D. (1968) *Minutes of the Meeting of the New York Psychoanalytic Institute and Society, Nov. 12, 1968*. The use of an object, by D. W. Winnicott [Summary of discussion]. Unpublished minutes.

Newman, A. (1989) Destruction as achievement. Squiggle Foundation Lecture, 4 March 1989.

Newman, A., Mitchell, J. & Kohon, G. (1987) What is good is always being destroyed. Squiggle Foundation Public Lecture, 17 October 1987.

Ogden, T. H. (1986) *The Matrix of the Mind: Object Relations and the Psychoanalytic Dialogue*, New York: Jason Aronson.

Ogden, T. H. (1989) *The Primitive Edge of Experience*, Northvale, NJ: Jason Aronson.

Ogden, T. H. (1994) *Subjects of Analysis*, Northvale, NJ: Jason Aronson.

Pizer, S. A. (1992) The negotiation of paradox in the analytic process, *Psychoanalytic Dialogues*, 2, 215–40.

Rayner, E. (1991) *The Independent Mind in British Psychoanalysis*, Northvale, NJ: Jason Aronson.

Rodman, F. R. (1987) *The Spontaneous Gesture: Selected Letters of D. W. Winnicott*, Cambridge: Harvard University Press.

Rudnytsky, P. L. (1991) *The Psychoanalytic Vocation: Rank, Winnicott, and the Legacy of Freud*, New Haven: Yale University Press.

Slochower, J. A. (1994) The evolution of object usage and the holding environment, *Contemporary Psychoanalysis*, 30, 135–51.

Winnicott, C., Shepherd, R. & Davis, M. (1989) *Psychoanalytic Explorations*, Cambridge: Harvard University Press.

Winnicott, D. W. (1935) The manic defence. In: *Through Paediatrics to Psychoanalysis*, London: Hogarth Press, 1987.

Winnicott, D. W. (1954) The depressive position in normal emotional development. In: *Through Paediatrics to Psychoanalysis*, London: Hogarth Press, 1987.

Winnicott, D. W. (1958) Psycho-analysis and the sense of guilt. In: *The Maturational Processes and the Facilitating Environment*, London: Hogarth Press, 1987.

Winnicott, D. W. (1963) The development of the capacity for concern. In: *The Maturational Processes and the Facilitating Environment*, London: Hogarth Press, 1987.

Winnicott, D. W. (1968) Communication between infant and mother, and mother and infant, compared and contrasted. In: *Babies and Their Mothers*, Reading, MA: Addison-Wesley, 1987.

Winnicott, D. W. (1968) Comments on my paper "The Use of an Object". in C. Winnicott, R. Shepherd & M. Davis (1989) *Psychoanalytic Explorations*, Cambridge; Harvard University Press, 1989.

Winnicott, D. W. (1969) The use of an object in the context of *Moses and Monotheism*. In: C. Winnicott, R. Shepherd & M. Davis (1989) *Psychoanalytic Explorations*, Cambridge; Harvard University Press, 1989.

Winnicott, D. W. (1969) The use of an object, *International Journal of Psychoanalysis*, 50, 711–16.

Winnicott, D. W. (1970) The place of the monarchy. In: *Home is Where We Start From: Essays by a Psychoanalyst*, Harmondsworth: Penguin, 1986.

Winnicott, D. W. (1971) Playing: Creative activity and the search for the self. In: *Playing and Reality*, Harmondsworth: Penguin, 1986.

WINNICOTT AND TRANSFERENCE: THE KNIFE-EDGE OF BELIEF

Laurence Spurling

This paper was originally given at the Guild of Psychotherapists' Summer Conference in July 1993.

> The mother commented: "How strikingly the use of the transference emerges in the knife edge between participation and interpretation" (*The Piggle*).
>
> In social work a man says to the worker, "You remind me of my mother". Nothing need be done about this, except for the worker to believe in it. (*Counter-transference*).

Freud's discovery or invention of the transference—it is not clear how much the idea of transference was created by Freud or lying around waiting to be found—was his most original contribution to the practice of psychotherapy. In Winnicott's own vision of the transference experience we can find most graphically revealed the style and direction of his work and his thinking. In fact Winnicott had little to say specifically about transference. His one contribution was to emphasise a distinction between the transference in borderline and psychotic states as opposed to neurotic ones, the former having a more immediate primary process quality to it. Rather than pursue this line of thinking, I want rather to try to dig out of Winnicott's work a more general and substantive conception of transference.

I have chosen to approach this task by taking a vignette of Winnicott's as an illustration of his use of the transference, although this is not what it is specifically about. The vignette is from a paper called "The importance of the setting in meeting regression in psycho-analysis", which was written for a seminar given to third-year students at the Institute of Psycho-Analysis in 1964. In such a paper, given not to his colleagues but to students, one might expect Winnicott to be less guarded in his exposition.

In illustration I will give a detail in the analysis of a patient who has a tremendous area of healthy personality and yet her analysis inevitably leads to this very deep dependence which is so dangerous. She is past the point of no return.

This patient comes into my room on a Friday, Friday being a day for cashing in on the work of the week. In this patient the pattern of the week is clearly set and Friday on this occasion was to be characterised by calm after storm with some kind of preparation for the weekend contained in it.

In regard to this patient there are certain things that have to be the same always. The curtains are drawn; the door is on the latch so that the patient can come straight in; all the arrangements in the room must be constant and also there are some objects which are variable but which belong to the transference relationship. At the time that I am describing the constant object is placed in a certain position on the desk and there are certain papers which have accumulated which I put beside me waiting for the moment when the patient will want them back.

This Friday in spite of careful inspection of my arrangements of the room I leave the papers on top of the other object instead of putting them beside me. The patient comes into the room and sees these alterations, and when I arrive on the scene I find that this is a complete disaster. I see at the moment of entering the room what has happened and I know that I shall be very lucky if we recover from this disaster in a matter of weeks.

Perhaps this illustrates the way in which the patient becomes sensitised to the setting and its details. In another analysis there are alterations all the time. They may be noticed; they may be important; but they are not disastrous. This patient could not do anything about her reactions except to let them happen. After her initial reaction, which was unreasonable in the extreme, she began to become reasonable and eventually came round to asking what it was in herself that made people behave badly. Eventually she asked me to talk about this, what had she done that made me make this mistake?—a mistake which completely broke up the process of the analysis and of her development, and ruined the whole work of the week?

Before the end of the hour in this case I was able to talk about the whole thing in the way that she asked me to do, which is rather different from giving an interpretation. This is a favourable outcome, which one must not always expect. It could easily have happened that a patient highly sensitised in this way could have a suicidal episode in the weekend or could leave the analysis or could do a piece of acting out from which it would be very difficult ever to recover, like marrying the wrong person. I have had all these things happen in my practice and that is why I am trying to convey how difficult it is to do this work well. On this particular day with this patient I was able to say that as far as I could see this disastrous mistake that I had made had unconscious motivation. I could guess at some of my reasons for making the mistake but in my own opinion, I said, the mistake lies within me and is not a reaction to something in the patient.

I went on, because of the material I had at hand, to show that the patient would much prefer to find that what I had done disastrously was a reaction of something in herself, because this would bring the whole thing into her control and give her some hope for bringing about a change in me because of a change in herself.

From this the patient took the matter back to certain things about her father which she had always tried hard to explain as reactions to something in herself, whereas she had to admit that they were characteristics of her father dating from the time before she was born and indeed explicable in terms of his own family history.

In the end I was able to say: "The thing is, this is what I am like, and if you continue with me you will find I shall do similar things with unconscious motivation again because that is what I am like" (Winnicott, 1989, pp. 98-100).

Although the word "transference" is mentioned only once, we can see how for Winnicott psychotherapy is a continual enactment of a kind of theatre. Both patient and therapist take part in this drama, the therapist, as well as being an actor, taking responsibility for stage-managing the play and giving it some basic direction, although taking cues from the patient. In this particular play I can distinguish four acts, and possibly five.

In *Act One* Winnicott sets the scene, in which objects in his room "have" to be laid out in a highly specific manner for this patient. Winnicott then describes how he gets this arrangement wrong, leading to a "complete disaster" with the therapy, from which the patient may take weeks to recover.

What is striking about the way Winnicott writes here is that *there is no real separation between the voice of the patient and the voice of the therapist.* What is a disaster for the patient is *also* a disaster for the therapist. As the narrator of this story, Winnicott eschews narrative distance: he claims to know no better than the patient. This is a powerful example of Winnicott's idea of the absolute necessity for the therapist to believe in the transference. In his judgment, this patient *needed* Winnicott to believe that a small change in the "setting" of the therapy constituted an unmitigated disaster for her ("need" here is opposed to "want").

In *Act Two*, however, the tone suddenly changes, and we find that Winnicott engages his patient in a *conversation* about what happened. He gives his own particular twist to the event, saying it had been his mistake which had been brought about by his own unconscious motivation. In thus commenting on both the event and himself, Winnicott moves from participation to interpretation, from a kind of merging with the patient, in which it was impossible to tell who was sane and who was mad, to the taking up of a meta-position in which Winnicott establishes himself as separate from the patient, and also as someone *outside of her omnipotence*, in this case by emphasising to her that he has an unconscious to which, like all mortals, he is subject, and over which neither he nor she has control.

In *Act Three*, in which Winnicott shows the patient that she would have preferred to see his mistake as having been occasioned or caused by her, we see Winnicott giving a classical transference interpretation. By *not* acting as the patient wanted him to act, that is by refusing to take the role she had allotted him, he is able to speak of her wish that he play a part in which his mistakes are caused or motivated by her actions. Here we are in the realm of wishes that are to be interpreted rather than gratified, as opposed to needs that are either simply met or not met.

In *Act Four* the patient *remembers* some aspects of her father which correspond to how she had wanted Winnicott to act. In terms of Freud's classic formula, she is *remembering* as opposed to *acting out*, although in this case one would have to say that, if there was acting out, it was done by the therapist as well as the patient. Winnicott's own language would be quite different: he would say that the patient was sufficiently held by him, by his taking her distress seriously, in order for her to become gathered together enough in order to be able to remember.

Finally Winnicott rather rhetorically tells the patient that he is who he is, that he has an unconscious, and that he is outside her area of omnipotence. I think here Winnicott is asserting his otherness and separateness to his patient and inviting her, in his own language, to use him as an object, someone who is more than the sum of her projections. In fact, in the course of this session one can see the patient moving from a state of not being able to play to being able to play, from acting in a rigid and controlling way to a loosening up of experience allowing her imaginatively to remember.

WINNICOTT AND FREUD

Now this short example of Winnicott's approach shows him to be grounded in a classical understanding of transference. Like Klein, Winnicott sees the whole of the patient's relationship to him and to the setting through the lens of transference, as a means of gaining access to her inner world. Like Freud he sees here a progression from acting out to remembering and, indeed, he draws attention to the dangers of acting out.

At the same time, although the *language* of psychoanalysis is there, the *spirit* does not quite fit into the tradition. Winnicott's writing has a quite different "feel" to it from the usual styles of clinical writing. Winnicott himself comes over as *embodied*, as does his patient, so that we are given a picture of two people in relation to each other, rather than, say, the operation of mental mechanisms or the mapping of unconscious phantasy. His conception of transference, as revealed in this piece, has something not quite *kosher* about it.

I think this will become clearer if we look briefly at how the idea of transference came into being and why.

In the last few pages of his long section on psychotherapy in *Studies on Hysteria* Freud introduces the idea of transference as a factor that can disturb "the patient's relation to the doctor", which Freud had recognised right from the beginning of his practice always played a crucial part in the patient's recovery from illness. Freud describes this disturbance as the patient being frightened:

> that she is transferring on to the figure of the physician the distressing ideas which arise from the content of the analysis (Freud, 1895, p. 302).

He gives as an example a patient whose hysterical symptoms had as their origin an unconscious wish that a man with whom she was acquainted would give her a kiss.

> On one occasion, at the end of a session, a similar wish came up in her about me. She was horrified at it, spent a sleepless night, and at the next session, though she did not refuse to be treated, was quite useless for work. After I had discovered the obstacle and removed it, the work proceeded further, and lo and behold! the wish that had so much frightened the patient made its appearance as the next of her pathogenic recollections and the one which was demanded by the immediate logical context (Freud, 1895, p. 303).

Transference, says Freud, takes place through a *false connection*, in which ideas and feelings belonging to one person become attached to another, even though they do not belong to this second person. "Strangely enough," says Freud, "the patient is deceived afresh every time this is repeated."

Now although this is Freud's earliest exposition of transference, and lacks his later emphasis on the re-emergence of childhood and infantile rather than more contemporary material, his conception of transference did not fundamentally change. We can see this in Laplanche and Pontalis's definition of transference as:

> a process of actualisation of unconscious wishes . . .

> In the transference, infantile prototypes re-emerge and are experienced with a strong sensation of immediacy.

We can also see how Freud leads his patient to *speak* of her wish, instead of acting it out, and thus allows her to *remember* where it came from, i.e.assign it its proper place in her mind.

Therapy thus consists of a kind of *staging* of her desire to be kissed, without it actually happening; *interpretation* is putting this wish back into its proper place, i.e. the wishes, thoughts, feelings, etc., with which it is associated.

We can see what happens if this wish is acted out rather than staged in a description which can be seen as Freud's first recognition of transference. It was written in 1925, in his *Autobiographical Study*, and refers to an incident which is not dated but is reckoned by commentators to have occurred around 1892. At this time Freud was using hypnosis, but becoming increasingly dissatisfied with it because, as he puts it, he came to see that "the personal emotional relation between doctor and patient was [after all] stronger than the whole cathartic process, and it was precisely that factor which escaped every effort at control" (Freud, 1925, p. 27).

> And one day I had an experience which showed me in the crudest light what I had long suspected. It related to one of my most acquiescent patients, with whom hypnotism had enabled me to bring about the most marvellous results, and whom I was engaged in relieving of her suffering by tracing back her attacks of pain to their origins. As she woke up on one occasion, she threw her arms around my neck. The unexpected entrance of a servant relieved us from a painful discussion, but from that time onwards there was a tacit understanding between us that the hypnotic treatment should be discontinued. I was modest enough not to attribute the events to my own irresistible personal attraction, and I felt that I had now grasped the nature of the mysterious element that was at work behind hypnotism.

If wishes are acted out, therapy becomes impossible. Freud recognised that the patient is transferring onto him wishes that belong to someone else, but this third person is excluded, and may have to be excluded, as both the patient and Freud fall under the spell of the transference. The spell is broken by the unexpected entrance of the servant. Speech in psychotherapy, especially interpretative speech, can be said to be a more thoughtful and authoritative kind of servant, that which breaks up the spell of transference.

In these formulations Freud makes a revolutionary move. In place of the *physical* space of actions and impulses, he inaugurates a *psychic* space of thoughts, feelings and words. Whereas the physical space is made up of real objects, the psychic space is more of an *empty* space, giving access to the patient's unconscious thinking or phantasy. The opening up of this psychic space is occasioned by Freud *removing* himself as a physical presence; he now constitutes himself as a *representation* of another, as pointing beyond himself.

In this sense transference is not only a *process*, the actualisation of unconscious wishes, but a space, the space in which psychoanalytic psychotherapy takes place. Freud's own descriptions of transference as space were to liken it to a "battlefield", in which the conflictual dynamic forces within the patient meet each other, or to a "playground", in which the patient's compulsions are given free reign to assert themselves, in a definite field. Laplanche and Pontalis, as well as defining transference as a *process* of actualisation of unconscious wishes, also define it as "the terrain on which all the basic problems of a given analysis play themselves out".

However, having opened up a realm or space which makes psychoanalytic therapy possible, Freud's formulations have also given his followers certain problems to solve or come to terms with. The notion of transference is given an enormous amount of work to do, in that it refers both to a process happening within the patient and, at the same time, to a space or terrain within which both patient and therapist work. These two meanings find expression in different ways of speaking of transference: one works *with* a process, but *in* a space.

What is happening here, I think, is that the term "transference" has become a nodal point, a kind of cross-over which joins together distinct ideas. Somehow—and it is hard quite to conceptualise this—transference is meant to be both a temporal phenomenon (process) and a spatial one (terrain). These two dimensions are given different weightings by different thinkers. Freud's thinking is largely temporal: memory, development, death. Klein takes over Freud's more temporal conception of transference, but brings to it the dimension of space—stages become positions in inner space and transference becomes the mapping of inner onto outer. However, "space" in Kleinian thinking is neither the physical space of things in the world nor the living space in which we habitually live, but a curiously flattened out space, lacking both depth and perspective. The space in Winnicott's work is much more like real life, it is a space between people, a space in which things happen. Thus his conception of transference is more spatial and visual.

This tension between transference as temporal or as spatial finds expression in another tension: whether transference refers primarily to what is going on within the patient or between patient and therapist. Let us go back to Freud's description of the discovery of transference. In his account, of the patient's embrace and the unexpected entry of the servant, the key to his attitude, and in fact the hinge of the whole narrative, is his sentence: "I was modest enough not to attribute the event to my own irresistible personal attraction."

This sentence can be seen as the forerunner of the whole of Freud's writings on analytic technique, which he would later formulate in terms of the ideas of neutrality, abstinence, etc. If we start to think about this sentence we cannot help but notice its enormous rhetorical appeal. I don't just mean at the level of *motive*; that is, to wonder whether a truly modest person would draw attention to their modesty in this way. It is more at the level of *logic*: that the very idea of transference *demands* that Freud does not attribute the patient's reaction to his "personal attraction". Freud could not allow this, as he fought a constant battle against the charge that psychoanalysis worked by means of suggestion, and wanted to promote transference as something that had nothing to do with suggestion, i.e. was wholly a product of the patient. So, for example, when he abandoned the sexual seduction theory, he could never accept the idea that the reason all of his patients without exception came up with memories of seduction had something to do with the force of his expectation that these memories were there waiting to be remembered.

Thus the whole thrust of the idea of transference is both creative and defensive. It is creative in that another realm of experience is opened up, as important as Freud's treating the dream as "another scene". It is defensive in that, by removing himself from an interpersonal relation with the patient, by rendering himself invulnerable to her seductions, Freud removes himself as a living person from the scene of action. One result of this in the psychoanalytic tradition has been a discrepancy between, on the one hand, a rich and elaborated language of phantasy and mental mechanisms and, on the other hand, an impoverished language of relationships between people.

An example of this discrepancy occurs in Freud's brilliant and teasing paper, *Observations on Transference Love*, in which he advises the analyst that the way to respond to the patient's transference love is to find a way of working in which this love is *neither* gratified *nor* suppressed, by treating the patient's love as "something unreal" and to which the analyst is "proof against every temptation".

> He must take care not to steer away from the transference-love, or to repulse it or to make it distasteful to the patient; but he must just as resolutely withhold any response to it (Freud, 1912, p. 166).

This course of action, declares Freud, is one for which there "is no model in real life".

TRANSFERENCE AS PLAYING

We can now return to Winnicott, for, from his point of view, taking this statement of Freud's at face value, we would have to say that he has a strangely limited idea of real life. In Winnicott's language, the attitude Freud requires of the analyst is his capacity to *play* with the patient, to sustain and protect the *potential space* between the two. In *Playing & Reality* Winnicott wrote of the original potential space between mother and baby as a space created by mother, in which she is in a:

> "to and fro" between being that which the baby has a capacity to find and (alternatively) being herself waiting to be found (1971, p. 47).

This is a space of growing confidence, where the idea of magic originates. It is the space of illusion, a creative marriage of what is real and what is imagined, which, says Winnicott, forms the basis for our capacity to play and for the whole of our cultural experience.

In Freud's theoretical formulations, and this is true of the whole psychoanalytic tradition, there is no place, argues Winnicott, for cultural life, by which I think he means most of our personal and interpersonal life. From this point of view, Freud's contention that the analyst has to find a way of dealing with transference for which there is no model in real life— although it refers to procedures which are specific to psychotherapy, notably interpretation—illustrates a *neurotic* way of thinking. It derives from Freud's theoretical principle that life consists of the opposition between the pleasure and reality principles. Such a way of thinking excludes what Winnicott called the third area, the place where most of our living takes place.

This third area, a place of transition between self and other, reality and imagination, requires an ability to *see* this space, a particular kind of *sensibility*:

> I have claimed that when we witness an infant's employment of a transitional object, the first not-me possession, we are witnessing both the child's first use of a symbol and the first experience of play. An essential part of my formulation of transitional phenomena is that we agree never to make the challenge to the baby: did you create this object, or did you find it conveniently lying around? That is to say, an essential feature of transitional phenomena and objects is a *quality* in our attitude when we observe them (Winnicott, 1971, p. 86, emphasis added).

From this perspective transference is a particular aspect of that special form of playing, which is how Winnicott came to define psychoanalysis. As in all forms of playing, it is marked by its *precariousness*.

> The thing about playing is always the precariousness of the interplay of personal psychic reality and the experience of control of actual objects. This is the precariousness of magic itself, magic that arises in intimacy, in a relationship that is being found to be reliable (Winnicott, 1971, p. 47).

WINNICOTT'S VISION, HIS MEDITATION ON HEALTH

If we return to the extract from Winnicott's thinking about his work, we can see how transference is understood as a space of illusion which can be constituted and sustained only by the therapist's willingness to *believe* in the transference—this is the quality of attitude required. It is this willingness and ability on his part to enter into this transitional space—symbolically with this patient he is as much on the floor as he was with the Piggle—which, one might say, earns him the right then to speak of what went on.

We can also see that, although he uses the idea of transference as a process within the patient as part of his repertoire, the idea of transference as an arena, a space, is much more true to his thinking. Furthermore this space is far more of an interpersonal space than the classical formulations of transference would seem to allow. Against the grain of the very idea of transference, Winnicott describes real connections as much as he does false ones. Indeed, without some notion of personal or living space (potential space in Winnicott's language) there is nowhere in which relationships *between* people can take place. In fact what makes him distinctive in the psychoanalytic tradition is the attention he gives to describing real connections, which constitute the norm, or, in Winnicott's language, the "set situation" from which false connections or deviations from the norm can be read off.

Furthermore, I would contend that the whole of Winnicott's thinking is a meditation on health, on its manifestations—the capacity to play, for friendship and for cultural and interpersonal living—and its origins. His central insight is that health cannot be derived from illness, and that in order to treat illness one must know about health. Whereas for Freud transference, although of immense value, is still ultimately about illness—to do with false connections, deceptions, misrememberings and acting out—for Winnicott the point becomes one of seeing the health in this process, and from such a perspective transference becomes something radically different, something with potential.

This vision of health is uncompromising in Winnicott's work. For a man who loved to see paradox and transition in the phenomena he studied, it can come as a shock to realise that, in his conception of health and illness, there is no path from the one to the other. The difference between the emotional and cultural richness of health and the poverty of illness is a qualitative not quantitative one. For instance, either one has a capacity to play or one does not, one is either a good enough mother or one is not. Here there is no continuum as with Freud between normal and neurotic, or with Klein between the paranoid-schizoid and depressive positions.

This vision of health is also subversive. Although in his thinking and in his work Freud knew better, in his theory health exists only as an absence of illness. In a footnote in *Playing & Reality* Winnicott once compared Klein's notion of inborn envy with original sin; and, in this way of thinking, the psychoanalytic tradition does conceive of us as being born into some version of original sin (death instinct, envy, lack), to which, one might add, it sometimes seems as if only those of us who have eaten of the fruit of psychoanalysis have learned to accept and live with. In this regard Winnicott's thinking is heretical if not pagan.

Finally, I want to say that Winnicott's vision, as are all visions, is limited. When it comes to an understanding of borderline and psychotic states, what Winnicott offers is both vitally important and also unsatisfactory. What he does is to remind us of the potential for health in these states; hence his notions of true and false self and regression. And yet, although this is a necessary perspective, it falls short, I think, of doing justice to these states of mind. Pursuing ideas based on "foreclosure" or "perverse thinking" has more to offer, and here the Lacanian and Kleinian schools prove more robust than Winnicott's thinking, for whom the sheer *malice* of psychosis gets blurred, as though it has to remain just outside his field of vision.

> If I want to say that Jung was mad, and that he recovered [writes Winnicott in a review of Jung's autobiography], I am doing nothing worse than I would do in saying of myself that I was sane and that through analysis and self-analysis I achieved some measure of insanity (Winnicott, 1909, p. 483).

Transference, for Winnicott, is a drama of insanity set within the bounds of sanity, the therapist's if not the patient's. For Winnicott it is the sanity of the therapist that cures, although it is his capacity for insanity that aids imagination and knowledge.

REFERENCES

Freud, S. (1985) Studies on Hysteria, *Standard Edition*, 2.
Freud, S. (1912) Observations on Transference Love, *Standard Edition*, 12.
Freud, S. (1925) An Autobiographical Study, *Standard Edition*, 20.
Winnicott, D. W. (1971) *Playing & Reality*, London: Tavistock.
Winnicott, D. W. (1989) *Psychoanalytic Explorations*, London: Karnac Books.

A FIRST APPROACH TO CLINICAL WORK . . . "TAKEN BY THE HAND OF WINNICOTT"

Carolina Castro

This paper is about clinical material: my first patient whom I shall call Matias.

Matias was referred in July 1992 to the outpatients service of the Tobar Garcia Hospital (Buenos Aires, Argentina). He was 9 years old.

During the first interview his mother said the reason for the referral was that "he has behaviour difficulties mainly at school, he doesn't accept instructions, he has tantrums, he hides under furniture, he bangs his head against the wall, he hits the other children, he gets restless, he always wants attention."

Matias, talking at the same time as his mother, said: "Like a motor that cannot stop, I press the pedal right down and I start", (he takes a handkerchief from his mother's bag and blows his nose).

I asked the mother to leave the consulting room and I stayed with Matias, who immediately asked: "Do you have anything broken I could fix for you? I like fixing things." He took the plane from the toy box and said: "What is this, friction? It's broken but I don't know how to take it apart. If only I had my tools. . . . Some parts are missing, that's why it's broken! How do you expect me to fix it, by magic? If I had these parts; I'm not sure, but maybe. . ." He touched and left different toys of the box, unable to keep the continuity of playing.

It was difficult for me to follow him. He stopped many times saying that he was bored.

He came back to the plane saying: "The turbines will burn. What a joke! It's a toy, it can not explode."

We can say that Matias shows his broken parts and also says he doesn't know how to mend them because he doesn't have the tools to do it. What's more: he says some parts are missing, that's why I think it's time to say something about his family:

Matias was born in Rosario, the place where his family comes from. He has two sisters, one 20 and the other 24 years old. His parents were already separated when he was conceived. His father saw him when he was born, then when he was one month old, and since then he sees him at the most twice during the summer break. Matias spends his school holidays with his grandmother in Rosario every year. His father doesn't give money to his mother and he usually promises to visit Matias but then lets him down.

Going a little further with his life story, Matias lived in his maternal grandparents' house in Rosario from the time he was born until he was 3 months old. At this point, his mother went to Buenos Aires to work and he stayed with his grandparents until he was one and a half years old. During this period, his mother used to visit him fortnightly. When he was one and a half years old, his mother brought him to Buenos Aires and because she was at work Matias spent this time in a nursery.

Whilst living in Rosario, he used to sleep in his cot beside his grandfather; this grandfather is a very important figure, because the first thing Matias' mother thought when she saw him as new-born child was that he looked like him, and she also said: "All that he didn't have from a father, he had from his grandfather."

His grandfather died two years ago, which coincided with the beginning of Matias' behaviour problems at school.

Treatment started just after the first anniversary of the death of the grandfather.

One of the first difficulties I found was that Matias used to change his playing constantly: he sang, made jokes, played guessing games, crashed Lego spaceships that then fell into pieces on the floor, all this in an euphoric atmosphere without letting me participate in his playing. I couldn't play with him, nor make comments or interpretations: he made a lot of noise in order not to listen to me; or whenever I "dared" to touch one of his spaceships he used to say: "Carolina, put your hands in your pockets."

I was there to watch him playing. He used to test my attention with questions like: "Guess what part of the spaceship is missing?", "Remember what I called the robot last time?"; or as soon as he thought I wasn't paying attention to him he would say: "Hey, hey, Carolina, look!"

At this moment, my role as a therapist was to be there, "holding" him with my presence, with my eyes, with my attention.

Working with a child with so many changes in his life it was very important to build up what Winnicott calls "experiences of existential continuity": the therapist was there, his box was there, he had 50 minutes each session.

Nothing one could say would be more important than the facts or the experience itself. What guarantee did he have that this new "environment", this new "object" wouldn't fail him again?

I think this is the most important aspect of the setting during a treatment: it helps in building the trust the patient needs in order to show the more regressive and defended aspects of his personality.

Based on this solid base of "experiences of existential continuity", we started a second period in the treatment, where there was more space for interpretations.

These interpretations were basically addressed to the manic defences Matias so frequently used.

The concept of "manic defence" is explored by Melanie Klein and also by Winnicott. Its effect is that when feelings of loss or sadness threaten to be conscious, they are immediately denied and transformed into the opposite state of mind: euphoria.

We can observe this during the first interview, when Matias says: "It's broken (depressive), how do you want me to mend it, by magic (manic)?"

These hypo-manic characteristics of Matias are very well described by Liberman and Waserman under the name of "Juego Festivo/*Festive playing*".

One example of the work on the manic defence is the following vignette of a session: Matias built a tower of buckets and said that this time it was different, smaller; I said that since he came in I noticed he looked sad, upset, as if he was feeling like a small child; he answered; "This is the Pisa Tower that is falling down more and more each day" and he asked me why nobody stops it falling down; I said that there are people reinforcing the groundwork to stop it falling down, and added that he might feel in the same way, that he falls down more and more every day and he would like me to hold him. He went on telling me about an alarm that seemed silent but was very noisy at the end; I said that he didn't know what noises or sounds he could make to let me know what was alarming him. He then started to reconstruct a plane he had taken apart in the session before and said: "I fixed it, who said it was broken? The word broken doesn't exist for me, the word sane exists." I told him that it's hard for him to accept that he has difficulties, that he is sad, and he prefers to think that all this doesn't exist. He answered: "Well, it almost doesn't exist" (the manic defence is receding).

Another issue to be worked with Matias was the role he was playing in what was happening to him, and here I have to stress that his behaviour problems were very serious. Matias used to get a stick and destroy billboards, he insulted and hit his teachers leaving bruises all over their legs. When the head teacher phoned his mother to tell her what was going on and to ask her to take Matias home, she said she wouldn't because she was working and it was the responsibility of the school to sort these things out. The head teacher was totally overwhelmed. He used to call an ambulance, he wanted to refer Matias to the in-patient ward of the hospital, and sometimes he would expel him—between August and November he was expelled from three schools.

So we started a third period of the treatment, focused on what he was doing to create his problems.

One example of this work is that Matias used to leave toys out of his box when packing up; I used to interpret this to him as his need to be cared for and told him that he was the one who left things out, but then he used to get angry with me if he noticed that there were things missing from his box.

This happened several times, until one time when a picture he made during the first sessions was lost. When I asked him what he thought could have happened, he said: "Maybe we forgot to put it into the box."

This was a turning point in Matias' treatment because he started to be aware of the part he was playing in these circumstances (even when he was still merged with me: "we forgot").

In another session he was looking for the lost picture, he couldn't find it and he drew a new one; he asked me to help him to organise his box and in doing so he remembered different moments of the treatment associated with each item in his box.

Mourning and reparation processes were set in motion. Matias was trying to find the "parts that were missing".

It was right after this session that a colleague from the hospital told me that she saw Matias sitting on the pavement waiting for the bus and she said to me worriedly: "This child is very depressed."

This was a difficult moment for me as a therapist because even though I knew that this was progress. It's very difficult to see a child depressed and sad.

I used to read again and again the paragraphs in the work of Winnicott where he mentions the importance of going through the depressive position, mainly in patients with manic defences: this was a way of holding to the theory, in order to be able to go deeper into these depressive aspects, and also in order to be able to hold Matias in such a painful moment for him.

We were in May 1992 and Matias hadn't been accepted in any school yet. It was very touching to see him coming to his sessions wearing his school uniform, singing "It's the student, the true student."

Since he could feel depressed and also held by the treatment, his tantrums started to be transferred to our room very slowly in the following ways.

He first begun telling me about issues from external reality. During one session he said he steals coins from public telephones; as he was leaving the session I saw a car on the floor. I pointed it out to him and he answered: "Why didn't you put it into the box?" I said he was careless with his things, and therefore careless with himself, as he steals coins from the telephones. He answered he had told a friend of his who is a policeman to stay close to the telephone in order to stop people stealing. I interpreted this as his need to be cared for, to be cared for by me so I should put his things into his box, and to be cared for by a policeman who would protect him from himself.

He then started to play games with rules which he usually tried to transgress; if I wasn't watching he would be tricky, so I interpreted this as his need to be watched, to be observed, to be looked after because many times he wanted to do forbidden things (I connected this with his asking the police to stay close to the telephone).

He then warned me to change the padlock of the closet because he had discovered the combination (it has 4 numbers) and he could steal things from it.

And he finally took things from his box or from the consulting room, which I used to discover with surprise once he had left the session.

All these episodes are described by Winnicott (1956) under the name "Antisocial Tendency" (and also by Liberman under the name of "Actuation").

These episodes got into the transference very slowly, as if he was testing my capacity to tolerate them. Would his therapist also expel him from the therapy like he had been expelled from schools?

At this moment I started to "fail" him, to "disillusion" him (not on purpose of course).

First because another patient touched his box and broke one of his spaceships; this made him feel very angry even when I admitted this was my fault and I apologised. And second because I had to introduce some changes in the times of his sessions.

Matias' reaction towards these two issues was not to come to his session for two weeks. He used to call the hospital, many times quite disoriented about the time of his sessions asking when he was supposed to come, but also quite angry, when one of the phone calls coincided with his birthday and he said to me: "Give me a present, you bastard."

Winnicott says that the analyst's failures are privileged moments during a treatment because, if there had been a good enough holding before, these failures introduce a gradual move from "illusion" to "disillusion".

On the other hand these failures are reproductions in the transference of the original environmental failure situations that are the origin of the "false self". But maybe these are too many theoretical concepts. So let's go back to how Matias came back after the absence of two weeks.

The first session he said he used to like a girl but he then discovered she was "a bitch, a prostitute". He said that whilst playing chess and each time I made a good move he shouted "You are a bitch, Carolina".

I pointed out his anger saying that he might feel that I had also failed him, as had the girl, and asked him if he thought this could be connected with the other patient touching his box, or with the changes in the time of his sessions.

During this period of the treatment Matias' symptoms were firmly established in the transference, giving him a break in the external world. He had started school two months ago, and during a meeting with his mother she said he got on very well with his teacher who also described him as a very helpful child, very interested in writing the newsletter of the school, with no difficulties in staying in the classroom.

Whilst I was having this meeting with his mother Matias entered the consulting room and showed us his homework. His folder was completely different from his work which I had seen last year when he didn't really have a folder but simply loose sheets of paper. Matias sat down and started to do his homework; he was showing the way his internal world was starting to be re-organised (as Winnicott says, to "integrate").

The same process could be observed in his playing; he decided to change the name of one of his spaceships from "Death spaceship" to "Playful spaceship".

Talking about this spaceship he said he was amazed by its resilience since it had stayed the same for months; he said it remained undamaged because of the "joints" it had. I interpreted that the issue of "joints" was a very important one for him, connecting this with the transference in the first instance and then with his history, talking to him about all the "joints" and "separations" he had had as a child: from his mother, from Rosario, from his grandfather ... he interrupted me and said: "The schools". . .

From time to time he made the spaceships crash again, but again there was one that remained undamaged; but his main playing was based on building snooker tables and pin-ball machines with wood, plastic bands and nails, with which he invited me to play. . .

This was the beginning of "playing" (Winnicott, 1971) as an area of juxtaposition between patient and analyst, where the analytical work can be done in a fluid way.

I was really enthusiastic about playing with Matias, on the one hand because I enjoyed playing with his pin-ball machines and on the other hand because it was nice to see the progress from his not being able to play to being very able to play. And my enthusiasm was so great playing with the pin-ball machines he made that once Matias said to me "Carolina, be quiet".

It was the "Children's Day" (1). Matias came to his session very disorganised: he had come into the consulting room before me, opened the closet and started playing with the toys that were inside. He kicked me because I didn't let him open it again; he was throwing toys to the floor; he said he would leave the session. He did leave, but came back immediately, half crying and complaining because I hadn't offered him any present for the Children's Day. I asked him what presents he did get and he said "only" a cassette of the Simpsons because his grandmother hadn't sent the money she had promised to buy a game called "Family Game".

Whilst he was saying this I understood "grandfather" instead of "grandmother" and I pointed this out to him. He said "How could I say 'grandfather' when he is dead?" So I said that maybe he felt that during the Children's Day he lacked members in his family to give him presents, and I asked him if his grandfather had used to give him presents. He answered: "Oh yes! for the Children Day, for my birthday and for any day; but my grandmother instead offers me half empty bags of sweets [he said this very angrily] and this is like offering one glove or one sock instead of a pair."

When this session was over (it lasted 25 minutes more than the ordinary 50 minutes), he asked to come the following day.

During this session he built a copy of the pin-ball machine he already had, in a smaller size, and gave it to me to play with. He spent the rest of the session playing with plasticine, putting his fingers in his mouth. At one point he farted and asked me if I could smell it. I said that he seemed to be telling me that behind the Matias who has tantrums there is another Matias, a smaller one who suffers a lot for many things, as for example what happened to him for Children's Day, and he would like to know if I could cope with this little child, if I would accept him even with his farts.

Going back to Winnicott, once the holding is granted it creates trust, so it is possible to set up the environmental failures in the transference (problems with his box, changes in the times of his sessions) and the patient regresses to dependency, that is, the period in which the false self originated in environmental failure.

It is important to stress that this capacity to regress always implies hope, hope that things can change and that this new environment (the transference) will not be a disappointment but will instead give opportunity for a new growth, an authentic growth of the true self.

The regression to dependency could be observed in Matias on his asking for more sessions. He also wanted them to last longer (to have two sessions of 50 minutes together). He made a list of the toys I had to bring him because he "needed" them and did not have them at home.

Another characteristic of this period of the treatment was that he didn't want to leave the sessions. So I told him something about his early childhood: I asked him if he knew how he sucked during the breast feeding when he was a baby; he said he didn't know, so I said that during one of the meetings I had with his mother she said that the first time he sucked, he didn't want to leave the breast so he had to be separated. Matias was listening attentively and said: "Was it really like this?"

I went on telling him that since then, he had always been very greedy, and that even today he had to be stopped whilst eating, otherwise he got indigestion. And I added that something similar happened in the treatment: he would like to come every day, stay all the time, he would like me to bring him more things, as if nothing that could be given to him would be enough.

In relation to the technique during this period of the treatment I gave Matias an extra session. His sessions used to be longer than 50 minutes and I brought him items he said he *needed*: glue, elastic bands, a small piece of plastic and a blunt knife. I used to make jokes saying that I would need a wheelbarrow to bring all the things he was asking for.

I can not find better words than Winnicott's to understand and explain this:

> With the regressed patient the word wish is incorrect; instead we use the word *need*. If a regressed patient *needs* quiet, then without it nothing can be done at all. If the need is not met the result is not anger, only a repro-duction of the environmental failure situation which stopped the processes of self growth ... an acting out of a dream may be the way the patient discovers what is urgent, and talking about what was acted out follows the action but cannot precede it (Winnicott, 1954, p. 288).

The most regressed and defended aspects of his personality, so diffi-cult and painful to be faced, being the little true self so hidden and protected (by this false self that so many difficulties brought to Matias with the tantrums), was now manifested in the transference.

During this period of the treatment my main question in supervision was how the separation would take place, because I was worried about all the things Matias was asking for.

I realized the answer was that I shouldn't get worried because separa-tion would take place slowly and I think that was right because just a few sessions before writing this paper Matias said to me: "Carolina, here is the 100 australes back." He was talking about a little amount of money he asked me at the beginning of the treatment because he didn't have enough money to pay for the bus fare.

With the question of separation in mind I had noticed that Matias liked to build models. I suggested to him that he start Occupational Therapy with a man, which he accepted enthusiastically, asking me if the man was old. When I asked what he considered to be old he said: "84, 50", which are approximately his grandfather's and his father's ages.

To finish this article I would like to comment on something Mario Waserman said to me during a supervision in the hospital: he stressed the importance of the first patients in the future of a therapist. And I think I was very lucky in this respect because Matias, my first patient, evoked in me many of the concepts of Winnicott, whom I used to read very often because I felt he could give me a theoretical holding for all the work I was doing with Matias.

NOTE

(1) "Children's Day": An important date in the Argentinian calendar, when every child gets a present.

REFERENCES

Winnicott, D. W. (1935) The Manic Defence. In *Through Paediatrics to Psychoanalysis*, London: Hogarth, 1975.

—— (1954) Metapsychological and Clinical Aspects of Regression within the Psycho-Analytical Set Up. In *Through Paediatrics to Psychoanalysis*, London: Hogarth, 1975.

—— (1956) The Anti-Social Tendency. In *Through Paediatrics to Psychoanalysis*, London: Hogarth, 1975.

—— (1971) Playing: A Theoretical Statement. In *Playing and Reality*, London: Tavistock.

AN ANTHOLOGY OF POEMS

Anthony Rudolf

INTRODUCTORY NOTE

Back in October 1993 I was invited by Winnicott Studies to compile a mini-anthology of poems which would be included in an issue devoted to the arts. I wrote a round-robin letter to many poets of my acquaintance, inviting unpublished poems on a Winnicottian theme in the most general sense—creativity, play, childhood. There was no obligation to read Winnicott: this was not an academic or professional exercise and I make no claim that the whole amounts to more than the sum of the parts. I ended up with the following fourteen poems, happily dividing equally between female and male writers. Ideally, all readers will enjoy all the poems but if any reader finds even one poem he or she likes enough to re-read from time to time, the job will have been worthwhile.

* * *

Penelope Shuttle	*Jobi and Jubsi: Baby Talk*
Aloma Halter	*The Mind's Arena*
Miriam Neiger	*Even in a Fairy Tale*
Gill Gregory	*Accommodating Andrew*
Frances Presley	*A Girl and her Shadow (Paula Rego)*
Carol Lee	*Sleep in the Dormitory*
Audrey Jones	*Falling Apart*
Peter Redgrove	*Ancient Girls and Old Boys*
Robert Friend	*Disguises*
Jay Shir	*Nadia*
Michael Heller	*Florida*
Augustus Young	*Pavane for a Defunct Infant*
Alan Wall	*A Mist on the Dyfed Coast*
Anthony Rudolf	*Breughel to Auden*

JOBI AND JUBSI: BABY TALK

Penelope Shuttle

But you know his friends did invite him to a party but all
his parents didn't tell him wasn't that naughty of his parents?
but first he landed all the gipsies' hats off
Jobi was a very nasty person, slapped his songs, but Jubsi
didn't do it
but from that he didn't feel quite well which he normally
does but Jubsi he banged his table and went out of his house
to plant his flowers a yes way
but Mr. Jubsi didn't know what he was told so an arm
came through the doorway and tickled him and from that
Mr. Jobi didn't know he didn't know nor why he didn't know
From that day he was drowned
his elephant had been sold there were not factories listen
but Jubsi was lessoned at school
Jobi didn't know he was being sold out he picked up his house
and so
he was all bashed from dizzy
but all also he didn't know the name of our dog
When Mrs. Jubsi came out of the water she said is
that my chest making all that noise?

THE MIND'S ARENA

Aloma Halter

I see you
stand in the centre space,
the mind's arena: a Coliseum
with gaping arches.
There are no exits.

Again you tense
against the furies of memory
for they'll race your bloodstream's course
in a circle stretched taut across sight —
your own arena.

Tame them! you're told – Tame them!
Match their strength with inner knowledge.
You recognize the scene: your eyes in darkness
and head sunk to the empty rows, gauging
your distance to the sky.

EVEN IN A FAIRY TALE

Miriam Neiger
Translated from the Hebrew by Anthony Rudolf and the author

In a miraculous forest
under a blue sky
I collected purple longings in a bag
like mulberries or raspberries
in a book of northern fairy tales;
later I'll deliver them
to your safe keeping.

But the wolf got there first
and now
by grace of his teeth
I am studying
psychoanalysis
and I realise
why responding to the forest
is forbidden
to mature girls
dripping juicy colours
even in the closed area
of a fairy tale.

ACCOMMODATING ANDREW

Gill Gregory

Thunderous lizards dart through hedge-holes
as snakes rustle and hiss in soft grass.
A bungalow and garden, hidden in folds
of a wooden heath, nudge a suburb.

A boy twirls in forests and caverns –
his sister dusts amber leaves;
he holds a secret of strangeness
in head and hands which jerk in seismic fits.

Lizards and snakes are his surprise,
he giggles as they crawl under skins
of tight green neighbours snorting horror
at this reptilian brood, a nextdoor nightmare.

Later she sees the boy Andrew
down vistas of surreal episode
of colour and clatter, movement and freeze.

The epileptic boy disrupted surface calm.
His shudders shocked and his fixed stares
held her cold like salamanders' eyes.
Returning to a meal, a game, a laugh,

she ignored his temporary leaves,
allowing remains to resound –
housed in her sprung body.

Greying, she holds on to his sickness
long after he's haemorrhaged from the the world.
She holds his looming mass of quakes
and tries to reach an accommodation.

A GIRL AND HER SHADOW (PAULA REGO)

Frances Presley

"What I most admire in a woman: silence??"
J.M. Barrie

the little girl stands
            up on her swing
arms   stretched   between the ropes

is she going to jump?
            how far will she jump?

underneath in the sand pit lies
            her shadow all frowsty and fubby
spilling out in circular folds

            non-specific like shadows are
blowzy colours permeate lines
                        dishwater across a page

pubic hair up on end
            a small green scream of labour

in the background another girl waves
            her shadow above her
                        sways with pain

the little girl stands up
            on her swing

SLEEP IN THE DORMITORY

Carol Lee

And how did you sleep?
the matron asked with her starched
uniform firing static at me.

Why should it concern anyone how
any of us sleeps
folding-dreamed or multi-nightmared
tangled colours or straight sheets
so long as we clean our teeth
before breakfast?

FALLING APART

Audrey Jones

    Falling apart again
    Never wanted to
    What am I to do
    I can't help it

    Life's always been my game
    Play it how I may
    Tell you what I'd say
    I can't help it

    Love's what you're supposed to gain
    If you're good enough
    Win or lose it's tough
    It's not worth it

    Give or take is just the same
    Seen it all before
    Endings are a bore
    It's not worth it

    Needs can be such a pain
    Tell you why it's true
    Tell you what to do?
    You're not worth it

    No-one can take the blame
    Easy come or go
    Tell you how I know
    I'm not worth it

    Hatred is just insane
    Love to leave it be
    All the same for me
    I can't help it

ANCIENT GIRLS AND OLD BOYS
Peter Redgrove

Taoist children on a terrace playing at school –
Actually adepts reborn by their inner alchemy
Into the child-paradise of immortality,

Playing at schools where the mistress is the view
Of the valley, and with toys
That are emblems of currents of natural energy –

Playing with water, with sand, or mud, or clear puddles,
Or spiders in spirit-houses or bamboo spontaneous
Wind-chimes, they wear
A special school-cap worked in the shape of yin cloud-fungus,

Which is the adept's famous fragrant cap. And so do you
After a morning at the hairdresser's; and because of the beauty of
        that,
I call wind and rain and marsh and river

And thunderstorm like children to join our loveplay.

DISGUISES

Robert Friend

Hunchback needs no doubled looking-glass
to see beneath the hump a back as straight
as any athlete's, Dwarf no stump
to stand as tall as any Hercules.
Jekyll endures the fiction of his Hyde,
Pinocchio the fiction of his wooden dress,
Frog the prison of his warty skin.
All know the self that waits concealed within.

What is Heaven? The Place, as Mark Twain tells,
where each becomes what he has always been:
Hunchback and Dwarf straight-backed and tall,
Pinocchio more boy that Huckleberry Finn,
Jekyll pure singleness as his dark double dies,
Frog a Prince kissed out of his disguise.

NADIA
(born ten days ago)

Jay Shir

> In her eyes   the eyes
> Of the room   whose ceiling
> is taller than peacock feathers
> and whose mind
> bears all books and music
> I am found   the sky
> of my eyes is transpierced and swallowed
> and made her floor,
> her great unmoving

FLORIDA

Michael Heller

> Surely you lived in the best place before you died.
> Your balcony faced the bay, not open limitless sea.
>
> Often we looked across water to the city's streets,
> as before us, in the west, the buildings lightened.
>
> And now, as if, from the fact of dying, a child's bright
> fears throw a curious light into dark gulleys of grief.
>
> A sudden knowing, opening fold upon fold of memory
> which had buried one deep. This morning, who to tell
>
> that stars had gone, that sea birds were on the rail?
> For whom to wake, only to be orphaned by images?
>
> Air upon air, with possessions packed. And look, a gull
> still sits by the sill of the dead parents' window.
>
> Who lives here? The bird caws from far outside us,
> slits wide the self's envelope. And out spills light,
>
> intensifying fright. Things shucked off? Crates
> for charities scattered about the room? To have left
>
> the fetal curl, learned how to depart. Window cleanly wiped,
> eye at horizon's edge, palms minute and sky a cloudless vacancy.

PAVANE FOR A DEFUNCT INFANT

Augustus Young

Many years ago
in a land of summer dresses
when mothers were no
different from princesses,

a sickly child shut
up in his room – outside, sunshine –
nothing to do but
pretend that he is dying,

embalmed in seabreeze,
shrouded in the heavy curtains,
shadowed by a frieze
of rodents in the skirtings,

the wardrobe ready
to take him in when death occurs,
inside a heady
atmosphere of powdered furs,

never taken out,
those hanging suits, and wedding clothes,
old uniforms, stout
corsages, and furbelows,

all the forgotten
livery of a time long dead
to wrap the rotten
remains.
A boy stuck in bed
wants the open air –
and not to suffocate inside –
dreams some headland where
a swallow-dive at springtide

takes away the breath.
The sky reflected in the sea
calls to him, Don't let
the body go so freely,

there will be the screech
of siren sisters finding him
washed up on the beach
(the phone downstairs begins to ring),

and the shrimplike form,
transparent too, and cowrie-curled,
like something unborn,
or something out of this world.

Empty house, seashell,
the echo, echo, inside you
is enough to tell
who is trying to get through.

Eiderdown on ears
can't stop the breaking of the waves.
All that ends in tears.
All the sympathy he craves.

A MIST ON THE DYFED COAST

Alan Wall

Children are stumbling from dreams
their cries like thin reeds rise up
out of the waters of sleep.

A birdsong accurately knocks against the window –
that blackbird whose saffron beak
and anthracite feathers
last night warped in the tide.

We still can't see him.

For the third day now mist swallows the hillside
a philosophic mist Giraldus Cambrensis had named it
with a dragon in its belly
(old books have had their dim plates scanned
holed up on the cliff here).
A boredom so monumental, he said
could scorch a whole meadow with one flaming yawn

should anything rouse it. Soothsaying poets
conjured the horrors to come
from the wind of its breath.
So write Giraldus anyway
five miles down the coast at Tenby
between his complaints at fish-tithes never delivered
from the awkward squad the Lord placed in his curacy.

We stand at the window and stare
at its mist-wings heraldically stretched about us,
shot to the grey of a snow-storm halted.

Our promises sharpen
to cut through the children's thickening clamour:

Tomorrow we tell them
tomorrow will be without doubt
clear as claws in a rock pool
And when that alchemist
the sun arrives
we'll strip this hill of ancient legends
push the dark leaves from the lintel

set out at last.

BREUGHEL TO AUDEN

Anthony Rudolf

Our daily work is touched by
as it touches
the seasons of the year,
is touched on by the seasons,
touched with.

You poets you
plough on
regardless.

WINNICOTT BOOKSHELF

A Psychoanalytic Theory of Infantile Experience
by E. Gaddini (ed. A. Limentani) (London: Routledge/Institute of Psycho-Analysis, 1992)

This publication in English of Gaddini's selected papers (with a foreword by Wallerstein) gives a larger public the chance to enjoy the richness of his thought.

Gaddini, who died in 1985, was President of the Italian Psychoanalytic Society from 1978 to 1982 and translator into Italian of Rycroft's *Dictionary of Psychoanalysis*. Coming to psychoanalysis via medicine, and deeply influenced by Winnicott, he was particularly fascinated by the beginnings of psychological life and the developing relationship between mind and body. This relationship is one of the three main topics focused on in this collection, the others being imitation and the formation of the ego.

The 1968 essay "On imitation" aims to distinguish imitation from introjection and identification. Gaddini considered imitation to be an independent process preceding identification, a product of unconscious fantasy dating from the first weeks of life when the infant perceives external stimuli as modifications of his own body. He argues that we can recognize a regression to imitation clinically when the outside world is perceived as a modification of the ego. Recourse to this imitative process occurs when the capacity for identification fails: the individual assumes other people's characteristics without being able to internalize and modify them. This "magically" acquired personality is extremely fragile and Gaddini felt that this kind of mechanism could be at the base of the "as if" personality.

Gaddini locates imitation in what he calls "the sensory area", distinct from though related to the oral area, with its introjective phenomena. This sensory area, the area of relation between mind and body in the very young child, is a recurrent theme in Gaddini's work and this book offers some of his outstanding contributions, particularly "Notes on the mind-body question" (1980) and "The pre-symbolic activity of the infant mind" (1984).

In one of his more suggestive and original papers ("Early defensive fantasies and the psychoanalytical process", 1981), Gaddini uses his profound knowledge of Winnicott's theory to make a novel contribution to our understanding of the beginning of the differentiation of mental life.

Birth is, for Gaddini, an extremely important event, and (*pace* Rank) not only because of its traumatic nature, but because of the loss of the stable, safe limit of the amniotic membrane and the uterine wall. This loss is one of the most powerful primitive stimuli to early mental functioning. It is in this context, when the child loses the maternal body as container as well as part of him or herself, that the "invention" of the transitional object originates. This separation from the maternal body leads to the infant's loss of an omnipotent self and the development of a magical self by imitation. This conceptualization is linked with Winnicott's (1951) concept of "illusion" as fundamental to the first construction of the self.

However, the perpetuation of the mechanism "to imitate for being" instead of "imitating for perception" (that is, perceiving the object is experienced as being the object) is a malfunctioning of the first relation between mind and body and can be expressed in early psychosomatic diseases. In his richly illustrated account of these diseases during the first year of life, Gaddini distinguishes between the times when illnesses, eczema and asthma for instance, appear and relates them to different moments of this developmental stage.

Gaddini thinks, following Bion, that the experience of separation, though it has a maturational aspect, can be catastrophic and push the immature self back into magical functioning through imitation, rather than using internalization. There is, then, no capacity to define the border between subject and object, to recognize our limits; the reality of being separated from the object is not to be borne. Functioning based on imitation then becomes permanent. This theory is a powerful one in dealing with regressed or "as if" patients, making it possible to understand deep and painful mechanisms not reachable in other ways.

Gaddini naturally views a good relationship with the mother as indispensable for the satisfactory development of the child. But the mother figure is not the only one the child needs. Gaddini was a pioneer in arguing for the importance of the father during early development ("Formation of the father and the primal scene", 1974). The father is not considered as a "second" object, but as an object with his own autonomy and specificity, whom the child has to confront from the beginning.

Gaddini also takes a fresh look at other concepts: aggression, for instance, or the idea of space or the hypothesis of the existence of a Basic Mental Organization from which stem all other kinds of relation between the self and the outside world. It is a pity that none of the empirical research papers that he wrote with his wife, Renata de Benedetti-Gaddini, particularly on seasonal influences on transitional objects, is included. Nevertheless, this excellent selection of papers gives a good idea of Gaddini's thought and will be useful to psychoanalysts and psychotherapists in the understanding of ourselves and our patients.

Maria Anna Tallandini

REFERENCES

Winnicott, D. W. (1951). Transitional Objects and Transitional Phenomena. *Collected Papers: Through Paediatrics to Psycho-Analysis*, London: Tavistock, 1958.

On Flirtation
by Adam Phillips, London: Faber, 1994.

After a brief introduction to the joys of flirtation—its playful sabotage of certainties, its entertaining of multiple possible stories—Adam Phillips first tries his come-hither look on lady luck in "Contingency for Beginners". Eyeing the purely chance happenstance of life with a view to its potential—rather than being put off by the assumption that causelessness must be terrifying—he finds in it the offer of freedom, of constant emotional renewal. Typically, he engages *en route* with Freud on the psychopathology of everyday life, with Proust on the entirely accidental effect of the madeleines and with Winnicott on illusion and disillusion, wondering, by the way, whether analysis may not be "more of a search for dreams that a search for insight". At the end of these essays and reviews on matters analytic (before he turns to matters literary) he remarks, in "On Futures", that "Perhaps the function of psychoanalysis in the future will not be to inform but to evoke". Leaving aside the question of whether the function of effective psychoanalysis has not always been, in practice, as much to evoke—to enliven, to awaken—as it has been to find out and explain, it is clear that one of the recurrent motifs of this volume is a questioning of the nature of psychoanalysis.

Thinking about Erich Fromm, Adam Phillips distinguishes between "common-sense analysts (like Fromm and Anna Freud and Kohut) and "bizarre" analysts (Lacan, Bion). Although his own sympathies clearly lie with the latter, with the "intriguing", the "exhilarating", he also acknowledges a role for the sensible, a need for comfort and help of a steady (unflirtatious?) kind. It is not common-sense that he cannot abide, it is "fixity". In the reviews of analytic books reprinted here, there is a recurrent pleasure in those that engage his attention with freshness and a predictable (for flirtation has its own reliabilities) dislike of anything that seems to him narrow, doctrinaire, not allowing of any space for play. Finding himself profoundly out of tune, for instance, with Phyllis Grosskurth's view of Freud's circle, he concludes that "Righteous indignation is always a sign that we are in need of a new description".

Arguing through Estella Welldon's view of the role of the mother in perversion leads him to suggest that analytic theory is often the double of the symptomatology it attempts to explain but that it need not be—if it leaves room for questions, childhood's questions. Reviewing the letters of Freud and Jones, he comments that one of the problems of contemporary analysis is that people still defend ideas as they were parents, adding, in a typically trenchant aside, that the child always "defends the bad parent more ferociously than the good".

His essays on literary figures are milder in tone, less stringent than some of his analytic fencing. There is more to be reflected on, less to be contended with; no "colonial" dogma to be countered and certainly no single analytic lens to be looked through in order to interpret. Rather he muses on contradictions—in Philip Roth's relationship with his father, in Isaac Rosenberg's use of the English language, in Karl Kraus's fickle commitment, in John Clare's need to hide expressed in the very poetry that exposed him.

Contradictions, overlaps, tangents, border areas, turnings around, these are where the seriously flirtatious writer blossoms. You think you know what forgetting is for—but is it a digestion or a spitting out? You're worried about why your students are failing, but have you thought what it might be that they are succeeding at by not succeeding?

It is a method well suited to the shorter forms of essays and reviews; flirtation cannot be sustained for too long. The flash of a single sentence can sometimes leave an after-image more powerful than the text around it. The exact argument of "Beside Good and Evil", its querying of the meaning and usefulness of these words, may fade, while the casual mention of the "unconscious complicity of object-relations with Christianity" may linger. But then Phillips himself points out that "most so-called insights" "turn up in passing"—and it is in its very passing-ness that his work excels. The merit of this collection lies not so much in any intellectual consummation achieved as in an attitude conveyed, an evoking in the reader of a reciprocal pleasure in dalliance. (And this may be why the language and imagery of flirtation has proved irresistible to reviewers).

If I am tempted, as I am, to comment that I find *On Flirtation* less consistently satisfying than *On Kissing, Tickling and Being Bored*, then a phantom Adam Phillips pops up to cry "Oh la Madame, satisfaction??" and I am immediately provoked (exactly as he described—the function of scepticism) to question not only what it is that I think I remember of the previous but also the nature or desirability of satisfaction, the value of consistency ("Consistency is compliance", Phillips remarks *a propos* Phillip Roth's demonstration of how betrayed we can feel when people do not consent to continue to be one version only of themselves). And if I find myself disquieted, as I do, by the circularity of having the book commended on its cover by someone whose work is commended within it, then I catch a somewhat steely glint from behind the author's fan and promptly query my own query. And if I say slightly querulously that, with the exception of "Contingency for Beginners" there is little clinical material in this book, then a giggle behind the box hedge lures me around the corner to see that it looks different from that angle, that there is indeed more than one way to tell any story.

The enticement not only draws you into the pleasures of the sport but is also very revealing of the rules that you didn't even know you were playing by until they were challenged. Questions proliferate, leading at best to a multiplicity of possible answers. Why, I find myself asking now, are my images of flirtation drawn from the past? Why am I tending to feminize them? What is book reviewing about? Why am I writing this?

One of the many answers to the last question is a simple one: just as Adam Phillips makes me want to read Christopher Bollas *On Being a Character*, Julia Kristeva on depression and Marjorie Garber on cross-dressing (and not because they are the only books he commends), so I hope that some readers will want to read and enjoy Phillips (and maybe, too, that some will guess that they would not respond to him—or not respond just at present). As well as commonsense and bizarrerie, analysis needs its flirty, tricky practitioner/writers.

Gillian Wilce

From Foetus to Child:
an observational and Psychoanalytical Study
by Alessandra Piontelli (London: Routledge, 1992)

Foetal development has long been a subject of speculation in psychoanalysis, certainly since Freud's somewhat provocative assertion that "there is much more continuity between intra-uterine life and early infancy than the impressive caesura of the act of birth would have us believe" (Freud, 1926, p.138). Now, however, the development of ultrasound has meant that intra-uterine development can be studied relatively objectively. There have also been important theoretical shifts within psychoanalysis which must assume some kind of mental life in the foetus. These include a wide-spread acceptance of the new-born's cognitive and interpersonal competence. Particularly significant is Wilfred Bion's (1962) work claiming that infants are born equipped with mechanisms for projecting primitive thoughts, arousing anxieties, feelings and phantasies in other people. These would include evacuatory products of sensori-motor activity taking place within the womb itself.

Implicitly or explicitly, Alessandra Piontelli draws on each of these developments and aims to explore the nature of pre-uterine life and its impact on the individual. After an introduction outlining the author's own background, this book is divided into four major parts. The first presents findings of foetal development from embryology, physiology and other disciplines. The second and third describe the author's own research which follows the development of eleven foetuses, four singletons and three pairs of twins, through the intra-uterine period up until the end of the fourth year. In utero, for both singletons and twins, regular ultrasound recordings were accompanied by audio recordings of the comments of the parents and medical staff present at the time. Together with summaries of the families and other background information, particularly salient transcripts are presented verbatim to illustrate persistent foetal characteristics.

After birth the infants were observed at home using the psychoanalytic infant observation developed by Esther Bick (1964) up until the fourth year. Again, information is presented to demonstrate repetitive themes and a striking continuity which applied in each case.

This is not a clinical sample but it illustrates the anxiety associated with observing foetal behaviour and early development in sometimes inadequate environmental circumstances. In one case the anxiety was particularly high. As a foetus, Giulia, a singleton, showed extreme passivity along with an apparent passion for licking and stroking her genitals. Her mother was also prone to passivity. She coped with the demands of pregnancy by returning to her own mother. Following a protracted labour and an extremely difficult birth, as an infant and toddler Giulia had a great difficulty in accepting separateness. She developed an obsessive if not addictive demand for food and a precocious sexuality. The birth of a baby brother harshly imposed some recognition of separateness upon her. Giulia broke down. Her parents approached Piontelli for help.

Part Four presents a moving account of psychotherapy with this little girl, along with accounts of the psychoanalysis of five other children, selected from twelve small children whom the author has analyzed in recent years. Each child's presenting symptomatology and behaviour in sessions suggested a deep preoccupation with inter-uterine experience. In each case parental reports argued that the pregnancy had been anything but straightforward. Showing terror of enclosed spaces or a persistent need to be one step ahead of any gap, the infants were now apparently reworking their own relation to the inside of the womb.

The central claim is to have demonstrated behaviour and continuity in a way which has implications for psychological continuity and individuality. In fact, behaviour is used to infer continuities of three distinct sorts; in temperamental traits such as passivity, in a preference for particular positions or patterns of movements such as licking and in factors pertaining to organising an internal world, such as intolerance of separation.

These differences reflect the use of three different methodologies; ultrasound on the one hand and psychoanalytic observation and the psychoanalysis of children on the other. The study would not have been possible without ultrasound. However, it is important to be clear about what kinds of links to mental life this method has revealed. Rather than presenting in a quantative account of movement patterns and other tendencies, Piontelli chose to give us glimpses of the foetus in situ through transcripts of what was said by those watching the screens. From these we learn that the same features were described over and over again. Many readers, like me, may find themselves feeling uncomfortable reading these transcripts because of the intrusive nature of some of the comments. This is partly due, I think, to anxiety stirred by one's own infantile curiosity. However, the transcripts also illustrate an irresistible tendency to adultomorphosise or impute full human characteristics to many things which move, even where there is no independent means of checking accuracy.

As Piontelli rightly points out, the repeated imputation of character in front of the screens may well have influenced the parents' notions of their children-to-be as well as Piontelli's. But having separate observers, for pre and post birth phases, for example, would not resolve the problem of "objectively" getting closer to mental life in the foetus.

The nature of the problem is apparent once the infant is born, when infant observation can provide a rich source of conjecture on infants' mental processes. The observational context is always fed by several sources of information, on intention, attention, feeling states and so forth, including reactions stirred in the mother and observer. This redundancy and the opportunities for cross-checking are not available in observing foetal movements in the same way and it is one reason why birth does affect the confidence with which one is able to impute thinking or feeling states in the tiny baby.

A slippage from describing behaviour to imputing volition is also evident in Piontelli's speculation that a rudimentary me/not-me distinction begins with the first movements which have been shown to co-occur with the beginnings of sensory experience. Piontelli asserts that it is difficult to understand spontaneous movement without activation and from here (on the basis on individual differences) assumes the beginnings of sentience. This is not justified. We do not need to ascribe sentience to moving cilia, for example, not to characteristic ways in which a pea pod splits itself along genetically determined lines. As Hans Prechtl (1990) has recently argued, highly organized, specific movement patterns emerging in the first weeks are generated as soon as minimal neural structure is formed merely as epi-phenomena, products of endogenously regulated neural activity itself. It is likely that movement in association with feed-back mechanisms does play a part in the development of self/non-self boundaries; but this locates the development in a relational transaction, which is to say something else.

Despite these caveats, the impression that something is taken forward to affect the psychological tasks of the neonate is overwhelming the extensiveness or directedness of repetitions. The repetition was clearest for Giulia and for the children in psychoanalysis, where Piontelli could experience the impact of the transference and counter-transference. There, the consistency provided by the therapeutic context allowed for the containment of immense anxiety, as the children came out of near frozen states which Piontelli associated with traumatic inter-uterine events or birth experiences.

The anxiety produced in the consulting room does not tell us what the foetus felt. But it does raise questions about the absence of necessary environmental contingencies through pregnancy or the ability to benefit from them. Perhaps, surprisingly, Piontelli finds little evidence of affects of maternal emotional on foetal development. That the foetus may be buffered against effects of maternal stress is reassuring and probably true. But the quantitative concept of stress does not square with the impression that there were great variations in the space for a new baby within each mother's mind. This points to the significance of the mother's phantasy life and suggests that the mother's containment of anxiety through pregnancy might be a useful concept in understanding origins of differences in infants' capacity to work through or overcome toxicity inducing events.

Finally, while many of the findings are relevant to pathology, all infants concretely repeated aspects of being inside. This suggests that re-enactment may be a necessary working through in normal development, raising many questions for future work. For example, in infant play, further research could usefully clarify the predominance of pre-birth themes. But a postscript is particularly intriguing. Piontelli notes that, despite the diversity, at follow-up in the fifth year, the particularities of intra-uterine life were present but no longer dominated, as all children had acquired a new idea about a space inside the mother. This is occurring at an age at which Oedipal anxieties are generally integrated.

Accepting that the space from which one comes is not, after all, one's very own may be a crucial aspect of this task.

Cathy Urwin

REFERENCES

Bick, E. (1964) Notes on Infant Observation in Psychoanalytic Training. *International Journal of Psychoanalysis*, 45:558.

Bion, W. (1962) *Learning from Experience*, London: Heinemann.

Freud, S. (1926) Inhibition, Symptom and Anxiety. *Standard Edition*, 20: 77-172.

Prechtl, H. (1990) Motor Behaviour of Fetus and Newborn, Paper presented at ATTI International Conference. Dal Nascere al Divenire Nella Realta e Nell Fantasia, Turin, 4-5. March 1990.

The Compulsion to Create: A Psychoanalytic Study of Women Artists
by Susan Kavaler-Adler. (New York: Routledge, pp. 189)

As a full-time practising novelist fascinated by the insights of psychoanalysis and ready to believe its wide and fruitful lands lie very close to those of art, I licked my lips when asked to review *The Compulsion to Create*. In it Susan Kavaler-Adler sets out to "examine how the creative process can or cannot be used to bring about self-reparation and/or developmental growth" in the "special case" of "women artists" and to see "what role . . . the father-daughter relationship . . . play[s] in compulsive creativity". Kavaler-Adler's main focus is on case-studies of Charlotte and Emily Bronte, Emily Dickinson and Edith Sitwell, glancing across also at Anais Nin and Sylvia Path.

So far, so enticing. But I soon felt chastened. It emerges from the outset that the author feels deeply hostile to what she calls "the creative mystique" which endows creative self-expression with "all kinds of healing powers": the artists themselves, she complains, are the chief victims of "an illusion of cure". She takes as a founding premise Lawrence Kubie's (and others') formulation of art as "a product of neurosis", though this is never examined. Nor is the possibility that Kavaler-Adler's four central subjects, only one of whom married and none of whom had children, are not entirely typical of female artists in their single lack of loving interpersonal relationships. For Kavaler-Adler, creative work is in competition with the analytic process, rather than kin to it and she wants to judge their relative successes.

The jury is in long before the trial has begun; by page 18 she has told us that "the creative process can never substitute for the containing and contactful presence of the external other . . . in the person of the psychotherapist". Acknowledging that the illustrious artists of her study "never occupied my couch", she compares their lot unfavourably with that of "the woman artist Ms.A", a dancer/choreographer whose fruitful occupation of Kavaler-Adler's couch is the subject of the culminating section of the book. In fact, these 356 densely-argued pages are simply extended proof of the author's initial proposition that writer, like physicians, cannot heal themselves.

In Kavaler-Adler's basic theoretical model, to which all but Charlotte Bronte of her chosen authors conform, the compulsively creative woman has suffered from a pre-oedipal stage failure of mothering, either through actual death, as in the case of the Brontes' mother, or maternal abandonment or depression. Typically, this will have prevented the growing child from a successful experience of separating from her mother and developing an individuate self; nor will she have managed to internalise the good aspects of her absent mother. Into this void erupts a father-figure at once omnipotent, intrusive and unavailable. He unconsciously assumes, as well as the full force of his daughter's oedipal desires, the devastating power of the abandoning mother-figure and the two become fused for the child in a tormenting split-off object most commonly symbolised in women's writing as a male muse, a Demon Lover or rejecting king. For Kavaler-Adler the creative process, in Winnicott's language "a transitional space realm", becomes a sealed world where creative women cultivate a fantasy psychic intimacy with the father-figure as a substitute for real interpersonal relations in the external world.

This model is well-fitted to the biographical facts about the Brontes, Emily Dickinson and Edith Sitwell, all of whom suffered in their different ways from abandoning mothers and too powerful fathers. Charlotte Bronte is deemed to have escaped the severest form of the problem because she, unlike her sister Emily, was old enough when her mother died to have lived through an adequate separation-individuation stage, so her problems arise at an oedipal rather than pre-oedipal level of development. For Kavaler-Adler this is why Charlotte Bronte was capable in *Villette* of creating male characters who go beyond tormenting omnipotence and female characters who can love, resist and survive them. Charlotte alone of Kavaler-Adler's artists married and lived with a man—though as she died a year later, one might think she did well to avoid it for so long. However, Kavaler-Adler contrasts Charlotte's emotional maturity with her sister Emily's lack of it, as evidenced in the unresolved demon-lover theme in *Wuthering Heights*, where Heathcliff and Cathy can only torment each other and die.

Dying herself of consumption at the age of 40, Emily Bronte never escaped from a symbiotic relationship with her father which Kavaler-Adler terms "psychic incest". Emily Dickinson similarly lived for and with her autocratic father, only rebelling against him in the symbolic fastness of her own writing; when, after his death, she was offered marriage by an older man she had long adored from a distance, she rejected the reality of an intimate relationship, saying "If you want the divine crust you must forego the daily bread". Edith Sitwell, finally, loathed but feared the overbearing aristocratic father who had poured scorn on her opinions and physical appearance; overtly contemptuous in her own writings of the rejecting patriarch she, nevertheless, unconsciously sought out a similarly rejecting and tormenting male through her long love-affair with the homosexual painter Pavlik Tchelitchew and Kavaler-Adler describes a long decline in Sitwell's creativity and personal happiness even as the world supplied her with ever-greater quantities of praise and recognition for her creative work. By contrast with her bleak accounts of the life-stories of these unanalysed artists, Kavaler-Adler's description of her therapeutic relationship with the dancer/choreographer Ms. A., in the final chapter of the book is one where the female artist enjoys gradually increasing personal happiness, becomes able to live with a man and experiences her creativity as more fulfilling and less compulsive.

What I found most interesting in all this were the detailed psycho-biographical accounts of the writers' relationships with their fathers, which might well have been expanded and Kavaler-Adler's suggestive analysis of the Demon-Lover theme in literature. If "The Compulsion to Create" has an increasingly deadening and narrowing effect, it is partly because its conclusions have been so unequivocally stated in its very first pages. For me the subsequent abstract passages where she insists on the conformity of each writer in turn to her theoretical model were much too long. Once the theoretical model has been set up, it is easy enough to see its resonances within the different frameworks of each life without Kavaler-Adler using her theoretical convictions like sandbags, bludgeoning all the disparate details into submission.

There is an over-insistent quality about the book which made me suspicious, as novelist. Like analysts, one of the questions we must always ask is "But what is really going on?" The dedication to the book has a curious ring. It is shared between five dedicatees. The first is Kavaler-Adler's father, "who loved me, who cherished me and who enabled my creativity to flourish". There follow three other names addressed with similar kind of warmth and then comes the last dedicatee, "my mother, who introduced me to art and dance classes". This is strikingly terse by contrast with what Kavaler-Adler says about her father. Could it be that the father gave love and cherishing, while the mother only offered art? Could that be why

Kavaler-Adler is so adamant that art is no substitute for real interpersonal contact?

In any case, most artists would probably agree with her, up to a point and then say "But there's so much more to this business of making art than you tell us". Quite early in the book she uses a quotation from Winnicott which I think is true: "A successful artist may be universally acclaimed and yet have failed to find the self that he or she is looking for ... The finished creation never heals the underlying sense of self".

The point, however, may not be so much in the finished creation as in the process of making it. The process of creating often feels very like the process of finding—or creating, or exploring—the self. Whether or not the artist takes away the gains he or she has made after the work has finished, the joy of the process is very real.

I think that the truth about Kavaler-Adler's subject is much more various and more playful than her account allows. Some writers would be helped by analysis, some would not. Some experience their writing as a compulsive torment, some as a compulsive pleasure, some as a pleasure, some as a job. Some have dreadful fathers, some dreadful mothers, some neither—though I do believe writers often write as such length because they feel they have not been fully heard. Some substitute solitary creative work for interpersonal relationships, some see it as a necessary adjunct to interpersonal relationships. Many female writers live with men, or women; many look after children or parents with only the normal amount of strain. Kavaler-Adler's narrowness of focus prevents her from seeing her subjects historically or politically; she seems not to realise that prior to the twentieth century it was even harder to combine the life of a wife and mother with that of a creative artist, so that there probably existed a real and objective, rather than imagined and neurotic, conflict between the two roles.

Lastly, Kavaler-Adler's insistence, natural enough in a therapist, on the desirability of individual psychic health prevents her from seeing that society is also a place where experience is shared but roles are delegated, or joyfully adopted. Perhaps some artists prefer to suffer gloriously and publicly (as well as privately) in order to express the secret sufferings of other—others who through the reading experience may come to understand more and suffer less. Perhaps the combination of rapturous and labyrinthine sorrow with the sheer pleasure and play of words, or paint, or musical notes, is sometimes irresistible to the artist, bearing in its secret shadow as it does the possibility of artistic impartiality as a substitute for the long hard haul by which women usually hand on their genes.

Maggie Gee

CORRESPONDENCE

Dear Sir,

Thank you for sending me a copy of Helen Barrett's review in volume 9 of my book *John Bowlby and Attachment Theory*.

Painful though it is, as an author one undoubtedly learns more from bad reviews than from good ones.

Helen Barrett makes a number of specific points. Perhaps the most substantial is her criticism that I am not fully at home, or conversant with, the literature on child development and the specific details of the "strange situation". I must concede that she is right. Indeed, I did have quite a few reservations when embarking on this project about my competence to write about child development and child care since my work, reading and research, is all in the area of adult psychotherapy and psychiatry. Secondly, my "scholarship": I readily concede that I am not a scholar and the book certainly wasn't written with a highly academic audience in mind. Nevertheless, I think most of the points made in it are backed up by references and substantiated by at least some research or clinical evidence. Thirdly, Barrett makes the interesting point that Attachment Theory is really a very diverse and vast field comprising child development studies, ethology and clinical psychotherapy. It was to the latter audience that the book is primarily directed, especially as it is part of a series "Makers of Modern Psychotherapy". My frequent reliance on the work of Stern, I think is justified in that context since Stern has the unique capacity of being both a psychoanalyst and an empirical developmental psychologist. Fourthly, Barrett chides me for not making more of Bowlby's idea of incompatible but conflicting internal working models. Here, too, I concede that she does have a valid point. Once again, I think the issue here is of culture and language. On the whole psychoanalytic psychotherapists, such as myself, feel more comfortable with the notion of an internal world rather than internal working models, but I think the differences are more linguistic than real. She also finds my literary and clinical excursions somewhat irritating. I am not sure how to justify these, especially the former. I think the answer is that the book is something of an obituary to John Bowlby—it was written only two years after his death—and his life and work did stir up an enormous amount of feelings in me which I wanted to communicate to the reader. It is for that reason that the only bit of the review to which I really would take exception are her comments on the biographical section. Clearly it would have been nice to have more space to expand that but I did feel quite happy with it as it stood and the Bowlby family has also been quite positive about that part of the book.

In conclusion, thank you for asking me to reply to the review and also thank the reviewer for her pertinent comments. I suppose, like people, books have a personality of their own and somehow Barrett and my version of Bowlby just didn't hit it off, which is a pity but it is a basic principle of Attachment Theory that if protest can be expressed and processed progress will be made; and I take this dialogue as a hopeful sign.

Dr. Jeremey Holmes
Consultant Psychiatrist/Psychotherapist

CONTRIBUTORS TO THIS ISSUE

CAROLINA CASTRO is a former Squiggle Foundation student who attended a course of the Foundation's Saturday seminars, and is currently living and working in Argentina.

RENATA GADDINI is a full member of the International Psychoanalytic Association and Associate Professor of Psychopathology, Faculty of Medicine at the University of Rome. Among her many publications is a series of introductions to Winnicott's posthumously published books.

JESSICA JAMES is completing her training to be a Group Analyst. She works in Hackney with pregnant and newly delivered women and their partners through discussion and yoga groups. She also attends births. She strives to improve her local maternity services and teaches medical students doing obstetrics. She is a group psychotherapist with Newpin, an organization for vulnerable mothers and their children.

ANTHONY RUDOLF is a writer, publisher and translator. He has just completed a book about his childhood, and a study of the French writer, Piotr Rawicz.

LAUREL SAMUELS is a clinical psychologist in private practice in San Francisco. She studied at the Tavistock Clinic and is currently a candidate at the Psychoanalytic Institute of Northern California.

LAURENCE SPURLING is a member of the Guild of Psychotherapists, and a Lecturer in Counselling at Birkbeck College, University of London.